THE WANTING COMES IN WAVES

A Year Without You

HEATHER E. TISDALE

Wild Mountain Thyme Publications

THE WANTING COMES IN
WAVES

To my Best Beloved. You were the best of men and I am so glad to have called you mine.

Contents

THE BEGINNING OF THE END

Forty-Five days.

That's all we had from hospital to diagnosis to death.

FEBRUARY

08/02/2021

Dear friends,

Thomas was taken to hospital last Monday with an extremely low red blood cell count and an extremely high white blood cell count. We didn't want to say anything until we knew what was going on because I didn't think I could cope with lots of well-meaning people asking me for updates when there was nothing to say.

After a week of pokes and prods and scans we have been told he has cancer again. At first it looked like it might be the return of the Hodgkin's Lymphoma he had in 1996-1997 because there are tumours on several of his lymph nodes, but they have also discovered a tumour on his oesophagus as well as multiple tumours on his liver. He will need a biopsy (perhaps several biopsies) and then a committee of specialists will meet to determine which cancer needs to be treated first. We don't know what that will entail. Surgery? Chemotherapy? Radiotherapy? The nurse says it could be any combination of those treatments. He also has an infection in his lungs that doesn't seem to respond to antibiotics and he is severely anaemic, but these are the least of our worries.

It is day eight in hospital, but he is getting excellent care as far as I can tell. Because of Covid, I am not allowed to visit him. The signal is terrible, so communication is patchy.

I feel like my heart is being torn in a million pieces. It is so hard not to be able to see each other, but we are hanging in there. We are keeping it quiet until we get the official treatment plan, but we should know this week. Thoughts, prayers, and healing vibes much appreciated.

Love,
Heather & Thomas

13/02/2021

Dear friends,

Feeling a bit frustrated. We were told we would have an official diagnosis and treatment plan by yesterday, but it didn't happen. Nothing happens on weekends, so now we must just wait (im)patiently. The good news is he says the iron supplements for the anaemia are making him feel much better. I took him clean clothes today, but they wouldn't let me see him. I tried to plead my case with the nurse, but she was very strict and said no. It's his birthday today. Fifty-two years old. Nobody should have to spend their birthday alone in hospital. The whole thing is horrible, but it will be less horrible when we have a treatment plan to focus on.

Love,
Heather & Thomas

17/02/2021

Dear friends,

Breaking news: a Gastroenterologist, a Haematologist and an Oncologist walk into a bar...sorry, a hospital room. It has now been decided that his cancer is going to be classified as a gastrointestinal malignancy and that the tumours in his lymph nodes are not lymphoma but are somehow an offshoot of the oesophageal tumour in the lymphatic system. They are working to narrow down a more specific diagnosis than gastrointestinal malignancy, but he will be treated by all three teams—Gastroenterology, (for the oesophagus) Haematology (because lymphatic tumours fall under blood) and Oncology (for the cancer in his liver).

They had their meeting of all three teams, and it was decided to start with chemotherapy and not surgery and so they plan to (hopefully, fingers crossed) send him home by Friday because nothing else can be done for him until we see the Oncologist. They will send him home with lots of drugs—pain meds for the pain in his liver caused by the tumours, and iron supplements for his anaemia. The Oncology team will be in touch shortly after he comes home. This a massive turnaround from what was said this morning. It has given us both so much more hope. Thank you for the continued prayers and healing vibes. They are clearly working.

Love,
Heather & Thomas

19/02/2021

Dear friends,

I just had a call from the hospital. The blood test results came back good, so they are drawing up his release papers and arranging transport to bring him home as they agreed it was bad for his mental health to stay any longer. Thank God. I was so worried because last night they were acting like they weren't going to send him home until after the weekend and Thomas had a huge shouty meltdown. I guess throwing a wobbly worked!

Soon he will be back in my arms, and we will fight this together. Our motto is: "We beat cancer before; we can beat it again." He will have an appointment next week where they check his red blood cells and if he is low, they will give him a blood transfusion as an outpatient then send him home. We were also told that Oncology will be in touch soon to start chemotherapy.

These days of separation have been so hard on us because they would not let me see him and my darling luddite Best Beloved doesn't have a mobile phone that we could video call on, so we were dependant on a Patient Liaison Officer to let him call me via a hospital phone for five minutes every few days. If I don't respond to your messages, please don't think me rude. We haven't seen each other in nineteen days so will be making up for lost time.

Thanks to the friends and family who have supported us during this agonising hospitalisation. And thanks to everyone for your love and support now. We would appreciate your prayers and good healing vibes.

Love,
Heather & Thomas

MARCH

01/03/2021

Dear friends,

We saw the Oncologist and unfortunately it is far more advanced than we were hoping. The oesophageal cancer has metastasized to his liver, lymphatic system, and his lungs. The most they can offer him is palliative care. They have said that based on how far advanced it is that no treatment can save his life and with the struggle with his extreme anaemia and this lung infection which doesn't seem to respond to antibiotics that we are looking at months to live. If they can get the anaemia under control and figure out the source of the infection and successfully treat it, they might be able to offer him chemotherapy or radiotherapy to give us a few more months together but ultimately, he will need to enter a hospice programme.

We will continue to support him more holistically and with nutrition to ensure that however much time we have left it will be good. We are not giving up and though we do believe that miracles can happen we are also realistic about the outcome we are facing. We do not want to waste so much time chasing some remote possibility that we miss out on any precious time together. If a miracle is going to happen, it will happen. We are hoping for the best but preparing for the worst. Our hearts are broken, but our love remains strong. Thank you for your continued love and support.

Love,
Heather &Thomas

03/03/2021

Dear friends,

The patient transport ambulance just picked up Thomas to take him to hospital for two bags of blood transfusions which should give him a bit more energy and help him not be so mentally foggy. Each bag of blood takes four hours to administer so I won't see him until tonight. This was all arranged for us (including the transport) since we don't drive.

God bless the NHS and their excellent staff. I am so thankful that we will not go bankrupt trying to make his last days comfortable. What a difference from when we lived in Louisiana and he had cancer. The year he was ill our 10% co-pay on our health insurance cost us nearly $10,000. We had creditors from Rapides Hospital phoning up threatening to have our car repossessed if we didn't pay.

But my big-hearted Thomas (kind and thoughtful to the end) was concerned this morning that they should save the blood for someone who really needed it since he will not recover. He finally agreed that he should have it so we could have more and better time together. But as always, he was thinking about other people's needs. This is why I love him so.

Love,
Heather & Thomas

09/03/2021

Dear friends,

We have had an incredibly difficult three days trying to get the right pain relief for him so he could sleep but today we were given liquid morphine and he seems better. Can I say how thankful I am for liquid morphine? He is out of agonising pain (now just mild discomfort) and was able to sleep lying down for several hours—something he hasn't been able to do since Saturday.

We have finally been referred to the Palliative Care Services that get you practical help after the Oncologist thought our GP should have done it and our GP thought that the Oncology team had done it since they were the ones who said he needed palliative care. Why do they make it so difficult? I suspect the pandemic makes it harder. Thankfully, we are now in the system and can't move for support.

We were visited by a Palliative Care Nurse who assessed him and agreed with me that he is too weak to attend his follow-up Oncology appointment on Monday because he cannot get down the stairs so we will do his Oncology assessment over the phone.

We have someone getting us financial support with PIP (Personal Independence Payment) to cover his loss of wages and a Macmillan Grant to help pay for carers when we need them.

A lady came round yesterday from Occupational Therapy to order some mobility aids to make it easier for him to get around the house. We had a very scary moment the other day when I had to lift him out of the bath as he did not have the strength. She said there was enough space for a hospital bed in our bedroom which will make nights much better. Now I just have to move all the furniture out to make room!

The District Nurse just left. She is getting us more liquid forms of medicine as pills are getting too hard to swallow. She also gave us a direct hotline to call if we need help out-of-hours which had been a worry for me. I wish we didn't have to use these services, but I am so glad the support is there.

Love,
Heather & Thomas

10/03/2021

Dear friends,

My Best Beloved is struggling to let go. To let go of routine. To let go of normality. To let go of living. Every day he has insisted I put the laptop on his lap so he can "get some work done." I do, but then his body takes over and he sleeps with gasping breaths comforted by the weight of the laptop on his lap because it feels normal. He awakes occasionally, moves the cursor, and then falls back asleep.

Today the nurse and I got him sitting up since I promised he could sit up during the day and lie down at night. I brought him the laptop and he started to cry. "What's the use?" he said. "It is just pretend. I can't stay awake to use it." It made me both sad and relieved that he might be beginning to accept that he is winding down. We talked about giving in to that rest and not fighting it which made him cry again. But then I thought to read him a passage from the book *Quaker Advices and Queries* because I thought would help:

Every stage of our lives offers fresh opportunities. Responding to divine guidance, try to discern the right time to undertake or relinquish responsibilities without undue pride or guilt. Attend to what love requires of you, which may not be great busyness.

Love,
Heather & Thomas

13/03/2021

Dear friends,

We seem awash in emotions today. This is such a difficult time in our lives and yet it is one that we will all face one day. When you are in a long-term relationship it is inevitable that one of you dies first. I take my wedding vows seriously and am glad (despite the pain) to care for him now. I am glad I have memories of good times to hold me up and this too will become a page in our book.

We are both exhausted today from the struggle of letting go—him to let go of life and me to let go of him. We are both filled with frustration—him in a fog of confusion and me not knowing how to make him feel more secure. But the one thing we have is love. He is so keenly aware that his body is giving up that it is painful to see him in such distress. He just keeps crying saying, "I want to be me again," and "I am afraid I will forget I love you," which breaks my heart.

We had a home visit from his GP and a nurse is coming to help us tonight. The hoarseness of his voice is getting more pronounced, and he gets the hiccups a lot but that is normal for oesophageal cancer.

He is not in pain and if he is I have liquid morphine at the ready as well as the "just in case bag" which contains injectable drugs to make him comfortable. All I need to do is phone the acute care hotline and someone will come out and inject him with the medications. He is mostly sleeping now.

Keep us in your prayers.

Love,
Heather & Thomas

14/03/2021

Dear friends,

We have entered Upsy-Downsy land.

There have been tears on both sides this afternoon as we struggle to communicate.

"Are you thirsty?" I ask.

Yes, he nods.

I go and fill the cup quite full as experience has taught me the fuller it is the more water he is likely to be able to drink. Experience also tells me that I must lay a towel over his chest because the tremors in his hand can make the brimming cup splash over. I bring it to him all the while praying he will let me help steady the cup because I know he wants to do it himself. His eyes flash angrily at me. "I said YES I wanted water. Why did you bring me the cup?"

Ah. He means no.

This morning he insisted that he wanted to sit up during the day and lie down at night. I see him cross and fractious and think he is tired. He angrily states, "I want to sit up." I try to explain that he is sitting up and he says, "Why won't you let me sit up?" I hold my breath and try to understand what he is asking me. I tentatively say,

"Do you want to be on your side?" "Yes. I told you I need to sit up. Why won't you help me? " He starts to cry.

Ah. He needs to lie down.

So, I remove the cushion nest that was propping him up and I lay a few pillows for his sweet head. I help him manoeuvre to a horizontal position and he looks at me and says, "Am I awake or am I asleep? I can't tell anymore." I whisper that he is awake now but soon he will be asleep. I tuck him in and then silently weep beside him. I feel his anguish as he struggles to think while getting increasingly muddled. I feel my anguish as I watch him be less of the Thomas I know so well with every passing minute.

I lie beside him in the dark, tears coursing down my face as I watch him sink into what I hope is a peaceful sleep.

Love,
Heather & Thomas

15/03/2021

Dear friends,

He seems to sleep well for about four hour increments and then wakes disoriented and disagreeable. My Best Beloved was never a good patient (the common cold made him like a bear who growled at you if you offered him a tissue or said "bless you" after a sneeze) so it is comforting for him to be so grumpy as that it is his normal behaviour when sick.

Every day I see things fall away. The last time he ate was Friday lunchtime. He showed no interest in it and drank the red fruit smoothie half-heartedly through a straw (refusing to let me hold the container because "I am not an invalid!") but the tremors in his hand caused it to drop and the sofa, the carpet and both of us were baptized with red slush. That night we tried some soup, and he just couldn't manage a bite and said he wasn't hungry and hasn't been hungry since.

In the beginning he was drinking orange squash but said it tasted bad in his mouth and so we switched to cool clear water. Which after the red smoothie incident I was glad because water is easier to clean if it spills. On Saturday he could drink with a straw and would hold the cup himself and glare at me while my hand hovered nearby like an anxious hummingbird waiting to catch the cup if it should tumble from his grasp. This morning we tried the straw and overnight he had lost the ability to use it and so we have gone back to sips. He refuses to use a sippy cup knocking it out of my hand and shouting, "Don't treat me like a baby!"

He woke me at midnight asking for water. I filled the paper cup (as everything else we had was too heavy and breakable) and we tried some sips. He is losing the ability to swallow which is normal as death approaches but made quicker by the tumour in his oesophagus. I watched him painstakingly take a sip and observed his throat dance up and down trying to make the water slide down. With a cough the sip goes down. It took twenty-nine seconds to be swallowed. I counted. He took three more sips, and each sip took longer than the last. The last one took thirty-five seconds. Like Cindy Lou Who I put him to bed after his drink and patted him on his head and kissed his brow.

He has lost so much over the weekend but at least he is still a grumpy patient. I am glad because that part seems like his old self, if only for a moment.

Love,
Heather & Thomas

16/03/2021

Dear friends,

Relief is at hand for both of us. His GP did a home visit and said it was time for a syringe driver which is a battery-powered pump that delivers a continuous cocktail of drugs for pain relief and agitation, and my Best Beloved will be peaceful now and not restless or sad or angry. All those big feelings will wash away.

A lovely team of angel nurses came and got him set up and I cried a fountain and washed away all the tension I was holding trying to help him feel loved and supported. It is a comfort knowing that he will not be hurting physically or mentally from now until the end. We are beyond blessed with so much care.

We are peaceful together as we move towards the end.

Love,
Heather & Thomas

17/03/2021

Dear friends,

My Best Beloved has shuffled off this mortal coil, stretched out his hand and touched the face of God.

It was a very peaceful night. We were blessed with an angel of a Marie Curie nurse who sat watch over my Beloved so that I could get some proper rest in another room.

She woke me in the early hours, and I went to him. I held him close and told him our story—how we met, how we loved and how he died. I told him that now was the time to let go and be healed. I just kept repeating the words, "I love you and I know you love me."

I sang to him the ballad that I sang at our wedding, and he took his last breath on the last note. I am at peace because he is at peace.

Thank you to everyone who has been on this journey with us.

You will give me strength in the coming days, and I take comfort that we will always be an ampersand—Heather & Thomas.

Thomas Roy Pitchford
13 February 1969 – 17 March 2021

18/03/2021

Dear Best Beloved,

I am back on my side of the bed. For your last days we swapped sides so that the nurses and carers could look after you better and ease your passing from this life to the next.

Those days felt so disorienting. Everything felt wrong. This is not my side of the bed. This is not my life. This is not happening. But it did.

One thing I learned on the opposite side of the bed was another way that you quietly sought to put my comfort first. Because of my long-term chronic pain issues, you have sought to make me comfortable for as long as I have known you. You have given me the better chair for the sake of my broken coccyx when there was a choice and have given me your jacket to roll up as lumbar support when there wasn't. Time and again you have carried my heavy bag as well as your own if I was tired, and never complained.

I discovered that if you sleep on your side of the bed the controls for the electric blanket are a hard lump that pokes you right in the shoulder. You have endured this for seven years and never said a word. I had no idea until I slept on your side. Another small kindness you have done that I wasn't even aware of. I wonder how many more I will discover.

This morning, being back on my side—the comfortable side—I awoke from a heavy and dreamless sleep, the feeling of cobwebs in my eyes, and I instinctively reached out my hand to you. Even with my eyes closed I know exactly how to make that connection with your warm back. I know the exact sound you make—a sighing smile—as our skin touches. But today I opened my eyes, and you were gone.

But I take comfort in my comfort knowing that you were always thinking of me.

All my love,
Heather

19/03/2021

Dear Best Beloved,

For the first time in my life, I really understand the phrase "it feels like I have been through the wringer."

I have cried an ocean of tears as we had lots of lovely cards from friends and your death certificates arrived in the post. It feels so final to see things in print.

I went today to make arrangements at the funeral home. We chose Co-op Funeralcare because they had a website that was easy to navigate, and their prices were listed up front. How many others did we look at where they were cagey about the costs? We also chose this funeral home because I knew where it was. I could easily walk there, and I wouldn't get lost because it is one street past the library.

I opted for direct cremation which means it is done without a funeral. You were very serious about not having a gathering of people due to Covid, even though funerals are allowed with up to thirty people. It was also cheaper, and you told me that I should do the cheapest cremation possible and use the rest of the money to help me with living costs. You were always thinking of me, even on your deathbed. They said you will be cremated on Tuesday morning, and I can collect your ashes a few days after that. They asked me to write a small blurb about your life that will be read out as you are cremated. But how can you be summed up in a half sheet of paper?

I feel exhausted. Limp. Wrung out. I thought I was okay and doing well enough and then I ran one errand too many. M&S Foodhall was loud—too many conflicting sounds all buzzing at me simultaneously—and there were too many artificial lights, too much overstimulation. I started to feel panicky, and I could feel my eyes beginning to well up and was afraid I might just randomly start sobbing uncontrollably in the checkout queue. The mask was making it worse, and I felt like I might hyperventilate. I kept feeling like people could tell. They could look at me and think, "Something is very wrong with that woman with the wild unfocused eyes." Or that people would think I was mad. Or worse like I had WIDOW stamped on my forehead. I kept thinking, "Do I look different?" When people see me now, will they know you are dead? Would it be worse if they didn't, and I had to tell them?

I tried to hear your voice over the cacophony in my brain. You would have told me to have a snack or a nap. Or both. You were always much better at knowing what I needed even before I knew. Now, I will have to figure out what I need by myself.

All my love,
Heather

20/03/2021

Dear Best Beloved,

I cannot understand your filing system. I am trying to go through old bills and get to grips with our outgoings and the box appears to be filed chronologically by category and then it stops in 2020 when everything seems just shoved in haphazardly which is not like you at all. Perhaps you were showing signs of illness and I didn't know it because I never looked in the box (though I should have) because dealing with bills was not one of my jobs. I shall have to make my own system now.

I keep finding half-finished projects for both of us. I remember you complaining of being tired and not able to concentrate on the radio play you were writing, but we just thought it was lockdown fatigue and writer's block. I have compiled all the notes I can find and put them in a folder. Perhaps someday I can complete this story if I can make sense of your ideas. Why were you so damned secretive about your writing? Everything I ever wrote I wanted you to read almost as soon as the story was committed to paper. I needed your eye and honest opinion. But you, it was like pulling teeth to even get you to tell me what you were writing about. You said it had to wait until it was finished—until it was perfect—and then I could read it. Now, I never will.

I also found all the things I bought last year to make a green screen so that I could make a film recreating the video of *Babooshka* by Kate Bush. I bought the green sheet and the clothesline and the hooks for the wall to hang it on and you just kept putting me off. I remember how annoyed I felt when you procrastinated on hanging it up. I sat on the stairs like Medusa, my head hissing with angry thoughts that you had ceased to truly love me because you would not help me when I asked. I had finally found something to do to occupy myself during lockdown and you would not help me be able to finish it. But now I wonder was it procrastination or were you really unwell and we just didn't realise it. I feel quite sad now that I wasted time being cross about that but at the time it felt like you just were fobbing me off with excuses after I worked so hard to build that double bass and learn the bloody choreography. Sorry, Thomas.

It felt so quick—just six weeks—but maybe the signs were there, and we just didn't see. Or didn't want to see. I know it does me no good to play "What If." I know picking over the past with a fine-tooth comb does not change the fact that you are gone.

I just feel like I am dealing with loose ends. That I am a loose end—untethered without you to help guide me. I feel like I am floating further away and am all at sea. A sea made from my tears.

All my love,
Heather

21/03/2021

Dear Best Beloved,

Today is census day. I had been willing you to hold on until today, but you weren't able to.

I wanted a record that you were here, that you were alive in the world, that you existed. But now you don't.

I managed to fill in everything except marital status. I didn't want to put a mark next to the word *widowed* because ticking it somehow made it reality. Besides, we are still married even though you are dead, right?

All that was required was to just mark the status and move on to the next question, but how can I just leave it at that? Where is the box to write in more details? You have been dead for less than a week. I wanted to say that you were alive and wonderful and now you are dead and still wonderful, and your memory should be commemorated somehow in this census to say that you were important. But they don't want to know all that, so it was just tick the category and move along.

All my love,
Heather

Dear Best Beloved,

I read a term today for all the administrative paperwork you must do after someone dies: SADMIN—a portmanteau of SAD and ADMIN. It is fitting.

Every day I try to do a little bit of Sadmin. Too much and I become overwhelmed and cry. I do just enough to feel one step braver in navigating this new normal that has been unwillingly thrust upon me.

One of your last wishes was that I be able to learn to live independently. We have been a team for so long—more than half my life—and so much of what we did was together that I find it hard to decide things on my own. We talked through everything from the large: "Should we spend £800 on this cool pen and ink drawing by Chris Mould of an Emily Dickinson poem" (Yes, of course!) to the small: "What would you like to eat this week?" (The answer was always, "Whatever we can cook together.") There is little joy in cooking or eating without someone to make it for, but I am working on that.

We also had jobs that spared each other doing things we hated. I would gladly clean every toilet in the world if you would deal with things like contacting British Gas because having to talk to strangers and explain over the phone what was wrong with the boiler sent my anxiety into overdrive. Now I must do it all. With each phone call I make, saying words I don't want to say, I find myself less afraid but my throat hurts. Like the actual words are a bone that has lodged in my throat causing me pain. But with every retelling I am able to say it a bit louder. From a whisper to a scream.

All my love,
Heather

23/03/2021

Dear Best Beloved,

You were cremated this morning. I am glad I went for a direct cremation without a funeral. I know you hated for anyone to make a fuss over you. In a day or two I can phone the crematorium and make an appointment to pick you up. I have ordered the biodegradable urn we picked out and a small hand-carved wooden pot from Etsy made by a craftsman in Penzance to keep a spoonful of your ashes at home and the sort of necklace that is also an urn so I can keep you close to my heart.

It feels so strange to think of you as ashes now. Weirdly, I am comforted by the act of cremation as if the heat of the flames burnt away all the disease and decay of your last days. As if you are somehow purified by fire and like a Phoenix you will rise again in my heart and in my life as I strive to keep your memory—your goodness and kindness—alive.

I contacted Scottish Widows to make a claim on your life insurance. Scottish Widows—what a terrible name for a life insurance company. What was Lloyds Bank thinking? They offered a choice of a phone call or doing it online, so I took the easy way out so that I didn't have to say it again as my throat felt raw with the realness of it all. But even typing it in black and white felt like a dagger in my heart with every keystroke. There is no easy way to do Sadmin without reliving your loss.

I didn't cry. I wish I had. It might have made me feel better. I felt scooped out. Empty. Too empty for tears. Dried up. I curled up in a ball and had a nap. Then I woke and ate an entire chocolate bar for my supper even though I have perfectly good soup in the fridge. Even the act of chewing seemed to require more energy than I could muster so I lay in bed and let every piece melt on my tongue.

I remember the way you would pretend to be a baby bird and open your mouth as a signal that you wanted me to pop a square on your tongue like a chocolate communion wafer. I miss you and your silly nature. Nobody ever made me laugh as much as you did. I wonder if I will ever laugh like that again.

I still feel like this is not real, that it is one of those dreams where you know you are dreaming but you can't wake up.

I want to wake up.

All my love,
Heather

24/03/2021

Dear Best Beloved,

When we knew you were dying, we tried to make a list of every username and password I would need to know. You left me a list of things to remember to do because even in death you wanted me to be organised and not scattered. But we failed, my love. There are so many things we didn't think about. So many important things that fell through the cracks because we were racing against the clock—your clock—as your life ticked away.

I ended up having to open new accounts with several places because your login codes were taken to the grave. I swear if you were here Thomas, I would pay better attention so that more things would be a shared responsibility. I would do anything—even learn how to do it all on my own—if only you were here to teach me.

But you are not, and I must forge ahead without you. Every step I take independently takes me further away from you.

All my love,
Heather

25/03/2021

Dear Best Beloved,

I started writing thank you cards. I am glad I wrote down the name of every medical person who visited and what they did because so much of it was a blur. It all happened so fast.

It is hard to have to write the words every time thanking someone for caring for you in your last days. I try to make them personalised. I try to thank this one for washing you so gently and helping you retain your dignity or that one for coming in the night when you pulled out your syringe driver and were so agitated or another for letting me cry after they had to increase your morphine to sedate you and stop you wandering when you were likely to fall.

Each card is a reminder that you were here but now are gone. Your death is the reason I must now be thankful. And I am. Your suffering was great, and I am thankful it is over. I am thankful for the tremendous help we received and continue to receive. But now my suffering is great, and I am not thankful for it at all.

All my love,
Heather

26/03/2021

Dear Best Beloved,

I brought you home today. All morning long I felt sick, like I might vomit, and my skin felt sand-blasted from my bones. But the journey to the crematorium to pick up your ashes was a good one. I was taken by our friend Jo, and we had all the weathers on the way there—sunshine, rain, and a little hail.

There was paperwork. There is always paperwork. Whenever I fill out forms about you my crystal-clear vision starts to melt. The letters on the page wriggle like tiny snakes. But with a trembling hand I managed to write what was required.

You came back to me in a tasteful grey cylindrical cardboard tube. They gave you back in a matching grey gift bag like you were a present. I was surprised by your weight, the heft of you. You were so big you had to ride in the backseat. We saw the most stunning rainbow on the drive home. Bold and bright as if it came from Oz itself. It felt like a sign.

At home I found the weight of the cylinder comfortable and comforting as it leaned against me on the sofa. Do you remember when you got out of hospital how we sat on the sofa and leaned into each other to make up for the nineteen days we had been robbed of each other's company? It felt like that.

We watched the rest of season three of *Murder Most Horrid* that was still in the DVD player from before you left me. We watched together as I felt the weight of the ashes and pretended it was you. It is you and it is not you, but it gave me the first comfort I have felt since the day you left me.

I had a momentary thought I might be turning into Norman Bates, but I will do anything to feel like you are with me again. I am lucky I don't have to give you up to the ground until I am ready. There is no funeral, no appointed time to bury you. When I am ready, I shall take you to where sheep may safety graze and lay you to rest, but not yet. Just give me a bit more time.

All my love,
Heather

27/03/2021

Dear Best Beloved,

Going downstairs to check the post always seems to set me back.

There are lovely cards from compassionate friends (but less with each passing day) that make me tearful from their kindness. I am glad to have the support but hate that I have a reason—this reason— for people to show kindness to me.

Then there are the official looking letters. Anything with just my name. These letters make my stomach lurch as I know they will require me to once again write out the details of my loss and then find the energy to get dressed and leave the house to seek out a post box to mail my reply declaring that I am utterly alone. Well-meaning people keep saying I am not alone because you will never leave me but that doesn't work when we are talking about council tax as they don't count you. You stopped being counted when you died and now, I get to pay 25% less as a single occupant.

Then there are the crossover letters. Those are the worst. Letters with your name on them. Letters that don't know you are dead. Letters from places that I was told would be contacted on my behalf to save me the grief of doing it. Letters inviting you to vote or go for an ultrasound at the hospital or most annoyingly from British Telecom because I have already phoned them up and replaced your name with mine and they don't seem to have gotten the message. I know it is just crossover in the post—the letters were probably already on their way when I phoned, and the situation will be sorted by the next letter. But it hurts. Every letter through the letterbox is like a paper cut on my heart.

All my love,
Heather

28/03/2021

Dear Best Beloved,

Nights are the hardest. Well, it's all hard. Waking up, cooking for one, trying to remember the good times without dwelling on the fact that all our future plans together will never come to pass. None of it is easy.

But nights are hard because I miss the tactileness of you—I miss spooning you and feeling your skin against mine. Feeling the weight of your body, the warmth of your body. I can just about distract myself on this side of the house with reading or watching a DVD but crossing the landing to the empty bedroom is hard. I have experimented with embracing a bag of rice to see if the weight makes me feel like I am being hugged. It doesn't. Rice is no substitute for you and being held in those strong arms that could always make all the bad things in the world melt away. I can't remember our last proper hug. You don't know it is going to be the last one until it never happens again. Then it is too late.

Sometimes I am convinced I can feel you, just for a bit as I am dozing off. I think I feel you close by though the bed is empty. Is it you or just wishful longing? And so, every night before I sleep, I recite that poem you loved by Matthew Arnold like a prayer in hopes that I will dream of you. It hasn't happened yet, but I live in hope.

Come to me in my dreams, and then
By day I shall be well again!
For then the night will more than pay
The hopeless longing of the day.

Come, as thou cam'st a thousand times,
A messenger from radiant climes,
And smile on thy new world, and be
As kind to others as to me!

Or, as thou never cam'st in sooth,
Come now, and let me dream it truth;
And part my hair, and kiss my brow,
And say: My love! why sufferest thou?

Come to me in my dreams, and then
By day I shall be well again!
For then the night will more than pay
The hopeless longing of the day.

All my love,
Heather

29/03/2021

Dear Best Beloved,

There are losers of things and finders of lost things in this world. I am forever misplacing my good pen, my water bottle, my phone, or my glasses. You were always my sharp-eyed finder.

I needed to write my thank you cards for the day and could not find my good pen or any pen for that matter. I just sat here and cried because I couldn't remember where I used it last and was cross with myself because I am so careless. You would get so mock exasperated with me, but you always found the missing item while pretending it was a game show using your oily announcer voice to narrate your search: "And now, it's time for everyone's favourite game: Where's Heather's Pen?" You would follow up the announcement with cheering and applause from an imaginary audience and occasionally would shout, "Yay!!" in your best Kermit the Frog voice. Then you would kiss me on the top of my head and tell me you loved me despite my appalling carelessness.

I would give anything to have you here, even if you were truly angry with me for being so lazy and careless. I would take sighing and tutting over the silence that I live with now.

All my love,
Heather

31/03/2021

Dear Best Beloved,

It has been two weeks since you left this Earth. Fourteen long days of waking up without you. Not seeing you or hearing you. Not sharing ideas or funny stories or the workload around the house. Even in your last days you were worried about the impact that taking over your share of the housework would have on my chronic pain and let's be honest here, you did so much, especially when I was having a bad flare up. The pain is bad right now, my joints feel like they are on fire, but I don't know if this is a normal flare up or the effect of a broken heart trickling into all my creaky joints causing them to seize up.

I seem to be slow to notice things like I am in a Victorian pea souper of a fog where Jack the Ripper might be lurking. Last night I went to the other side of the house to the kitchen and suddenly noticed the bananas were ripe. Overripe. Black. When did that happen? When did I even buy bananas?

I decided to make banana bread. You love banana bread. I was busy mashing and stirring and humming and it wasn't until it was in the oven that I realised you were not here to share it. How could I have forgotten that? I don't know what was worse—that I didn't think of it before I baked it or the hollow feeling when I realised that I was baking to tell you I love you and you weren't here to eat it. I ended up eating half the loaf, hot and gooey straight from the oven, until I made myself sick. It was good, you would have liked it though I would recommend pacing yourself.

Oh Thomas, I miss you so much my guts ache, though that could just be the banana bread.

All my love,
Heather

APRIL

01/04/2021

Dear Best Beloved,

Some days I am a sloth who lies about on the sofa feeling like the Thomas-shaped hole in my life is a vast canyon that I will never figure out how to cross and other days I take tentative steps to start building a bridge and rebuilding my life. Today was a bridge building day.

I took some active steps to buy myself tools to help with the things I am struggling with the most. I bought a weighted lap pad made of the softest minky fabric that is used for kids with autism or ADHD or just people with anxiety. The weight is supposed to give you a grounded feeling (and I hope will simulate the pressure of a hug if I lay it on my chest) and the fabric has some little sensory bumps which I love. Like Lenny in the book *Of Mice and Men* I have always found relaxation and calmness from stroking soft things. Do you remember that restaurant in London where I liked to eat with my left hand while rubbing the flocked wallpaper with my right hand? You always rolled your eyes, but you also always made sure we had got a table near the wallpaper. I am hoping this will help with my anxiety and despair.

I also bought a body pillow as I find being alone in our vast, empty bed extremely difficult. I miss spooning you and the skin to skin contact from sleeping back-to-back. The pillow is about four feet long and feels like hugging a body. It arrived today and

I planned to sew a pillowcase for it tomorrow but about 9 p.m. I changed my mind. The whole time I was talking aloud to you, keeping a running commentary of my actions that sounded like this:

"I am just going to choose the fabric tonight and make it tomorrow."

"Alright, I am just going to cut it out tonight and sew it tomorrow."

"Okay, it is just two seams, so I could make it tonight. This is probably a terrible idea to start a project this late at night but—"

And then I could hear your voice so clearly. I could hear you laugh with a twinkle in your eye as you said to me:

"And yet....here you go."

And then I laughed and said, "Yup. Here I go!" and I sewed me a pillowcase.

I will figure out how to span the canyon that is grief, and you will be my bridge.

All my love,
Heather

03/04/2021

Dear Best Beloved,

I bought a lamp. A floor lamp, to be precise. I have noticed my already weak eyes have deteriorated without you. Everything has a hazy shade of winter look to it—all mist and chill and barrenness.

I have wanted a lamp for a while, even before you died. You with your sharp eyes who could happily sit in the near dark to read or use the computer never did understand my need for brightness. I would enter the room and you would automatically shield your eyes as you knew I would be asking, "Do you mind if I switch on the light?"

It was just another example of how you put my comfort first. You often played musical chairs with me swapping spots on the sofa to allow me to read under the brightness of the lightbulb and then letting me swap back to my regular spot by the radiator when I got cold. You never complained about that, only about me putting my cold feet on you as a signal that I was ready to switch places again.

But in the last year reading has gotten harder and harder especially at night even under the lightbulb. Hence the need for a lamp.

Because we are still under lockdown, the only option was Click and Collect and so I used my new-found skill of ordering online to order a lamp from Argos. I chose Argos because the shop is a less than ten-minute walk from our house and I would have to carry the lamp home.

Oh Thomas, I miss you and your strength. I loved the way you towered over me like a mountain and seemed to be able to carry anything with ease—the heaviest parcels or bags of groceries or even me. You used to lift me up in more ways than one.

If you were here, we would have gone together, and you would have carried it home as if it weighed nothing. You would have exclaimed a loud "Hee-haw!" and pawed the ground with your foot and laughingly called yourself my "pack mule." You used to say that is why I married you—to carry all the heavy weights. Now I carry all the heavy weights in my heart.

As I approached the shop I suddenly thought, "What if I can't carry it? How will I do this without you?" I imagined myself with a preposterously long box like a 2 x 4 plank of wood knocking pedestrians off the pavement like an episode of the *Chuckle Brothers*. I kept imagining their catch phrase, "To me, to you" as they passed a prop back and forth between themselves and suddenly felt over-whelmed that there was still a me without a you to share the load. I stopped to catch my breath and speak to you for guidance. Thank goodness for masks so no one could see my lips moving. I closed my eyes and pleaded for your help. I asked you to give me your strength like that time I found the strength of "ten Grinches plus two" and miraculously lifted you out of the bath.

I collected my order from the shop, and the box was small and light. I carried it home with ease all the while feeling your arms under my own doing the lifting. Then I figured out how to assemble it and now I can say, "Let there be light."

Let there be light to read by and light in my soul as I feel you with me, guiding me along the way.

All my love,
Heather

05/04/2021

Dear Best Beloved,

The expression is "there is no I in team" but what it really should be is "there is no YOU in team."

Oh Thomas, we were such a good team. We were a good balance of opposites. I was in the limelight, and you were always my cameraman. I was the dreamer, and you were the one who figured out how to make dreams come true. We both were terrible at maths and used to joke that we had one good maths brain between us. Though you were the stronger of the two of us which was not saying much.

For my fiftieth birthday you made my dream come true by making me a published author. I loved watching you watch me at the book launch. I loved the way your face lit up when you saw me shine. I was shining just for you. I hope you know that.

You did all the hard work on that book. All I did was the writing. It was you who did the research, the formatting on ADOBE, and bought the ISBN numbers. It was you who measured all the pages and set the margins using a complicated algorithm I did not understand.

We had such plans the two of us. A team of writers. We bought ten ISBN numbers because we were meant to share them out—five each. You were working hard on your writing, and we were going to publish something for you on our thirtieth wedding anniversary in 2022. Now you never will.

Before you died, we made list after list of things I would need to know, but we forgot a few things like where we keep those ISBNs, what is the pass key code for ADOBE to transfer it from your crummy old laptop to my new one (plus how do you even use ADOBE?) and how do you set the bloody margins on a book. I have managed with a great deal of effort to track down the first two things that I will need to publish future books. I am sure you were guiding me from Heaven because just as I was about to give up, I would suddenly think of a place they might be. But there is no help coming on the maths for the margins. Not even help from the spirit world is going to make that easier. So, I will muddle on and puzzle it out and swear and cry and wish you were here to teach me.

And every book I write, I will write for you.

All my love,
Heather

07/04/2021

Dear Best Beloved,

It has been three weeks since you left this world. I am doing better than I thought I would be. I am settling into a routine and figuring out how to manage without your help and your height. A step ladder has been ordered. I haven't quite figured out how to manage without your love, but I am working on that. People will say, "but his love will always be with you" and of course they are right, but there is a big difference between eternal love and the day-to-day love, affection, togetherness, and little intimacies that are now lost.

I am struggling with pronouns. Plural versus singular. I find myself automatically using the plural because we have been we for so long. Yesterday someone asked me, "Where is YOUR house?" And I replied, "WE live in Carmarthen." I roll the singular pronoun *I* around in my mouth to taste the word. It is not bitter, but it feels unnatural.

I sent an email and realised that both our names are listed at the bottom as a permanent signature. I ponder if I should remove it, but then realise that I do not know how to do so. Which is just as well as I don't feel ready for that. Saying "I live in Carmarthen" instead of "We live in Carmarthen" is a fact I can learn to live with but scrubbing your name from the email feels like I am erasing you from history. But then I don't want to become like a Dickens' character who has Scrooge and Marley above the door though Mr Marley had been dead seven years.

How can I still be a *WE* while learning to just be an *I*?

All my love,
Heather

12/04/2021

Dear Best Beloved,

We are coming up to four weeks since you left me. How is that possible? It feels like both an eternity and just yesterday since you departed this world.

I go back to work today after having been on furlough since before Christmas. I am excited about work which I know would please you. My excitement is slightly dampened by having spent the morning wishing you were here because I had to ring British Gas to report that we have no hot water. If you were here I would make you do it, but as you are not I must step up and be the designated adult in our house. I miss you, Thomas and not just because I don't want to be the one to have to call up and report a situation over the phone.

It occurred to me that now there would be no figuring out who would be least inconvenienced to stay home and wait for a repair-person. It will just have to be me. I am the designated adult. I am on my own here.

So, I add it to the list as one more thing I must be responsible for and carry on.

All my love,
Heather

14/04/2021

Dear Best Beloved,

Today it is four weeks since you died. It is also twenty-one years since my father left this world. There is a strange symmetry to your passings. March 17th was your last day on Earth and for him it was the first of the last—the day he entered into hospice care, and we began the road to his death a month later.

In the beginning I kept your ashes near me, leaning the tall cardboard tube against me on the sofa as I forced you to binge watch *Bridgerton*. I laughed knowing you would have hated it and teased you about being a captive audience. But I wasn't ready to open it just yet. But lately I have noticed the temporary vessel has been ignored. No longer are you sitting on the sofa by my side, but you are awkwardly left on the floor where I must step around you. I pondered what this meant. I felt I was losing you and so I tried to watch more Netflix with you by my side, but the weight of the ashes felt more uncomfortable than comforting. Maybe it is time, I thought.

Last night I could not sleep. I tossed and turned and could not settle. I suddenly had the overwhelming urge to open your ashes. I could hear you in my head whispering, "Surely this can wait until morning?" But I knew the answer was no. I was ready. I was ready right now. I felt peaceful and calm and was afraid if I did not act on those feelings immediately that they might shrink away, and I might drown in the tide of grief again.

So, at about 2 a.m. I got up in my pyjamas and opened you up. It was like opening a can of Pringles to break the seal and it made me laugh. It was good to laugh. I had a moment of just looking at the ashes—it is you and it is not you. I touched them. Soft grey with flecks of hard white. Bits of your bones, I suppose.

I carefully decanted you into your beautiful biodegradable urn. You made me sneeze. I filled various containers for various purposes. A poster tube to take to Llansteffan and a miniature jam jar to take to the Botanic Gardens to scatter. A bit in a Ziplock bag to send to your family in the United States. My little hand-carved pot. My urn necklace. The necklace came with a tiny funnel, and I struggled to decant a few flecks of ash into the miniature vessel. I spilled a bit of you on the kitchen counter, but I know you won't mind. I rubbed some of the spilt ashes into my skin to feel you close to me. I put a bit of you on my tongue.

At around 3 a.m. I was done. I did not seal the biodegradable urn with a dab of glue as they suggested just yet. I might think of some other place that you would like to be scattered and so I need access. In another month or so when the weather is good and warm, I will take your urn and bury you in one of your favourite places.

Each day I move forward with you and without you.

All my love,
Heather

17/04/2021

Dear Best Beloved,

I have noticed my vision has been very blurry. It looks like when I need a new prescription for my spectacles. There is a hazy film over my eyes like someone has rubbed petroleum jelly on my lenses. If you were here, you would be pulling that face that meant you were pretending it was you who had greased my glasses. "Oh, so you *didn't* want your lenses oiled?" you would say in mock surprise. Nobody has ever made me laugh the way you did. But it doesn't feel like I need a new prescription. I don't have the accompanying headaches and eye strain related to needing new glasses. It is just a blur. Like I am walking around tangled in a chiffon scarf. I can see, but I can't see.

I consulted my mother who said perhaps I should see the Optometrist, but I had gotten a new prescription a month before you died. So, I did what you liked to call "consulting Dr Google" and I found out that grief can cause a change in your eyes. Not your prescription, just your eyes. That refusing to focus was a normal occurrence after a bereavement. Some people even went temporarily blind after a shocking loss. Dr Google said it would get better with time.

Time is all I have at the moment.

All my love,
Heather

Dear Best Beloved,

It came yesterday in the post addressed to you. Flat and rectangular with a stiff cardboard backing. It was like all the air left my lungs for a moment and then came whooshing back in with a gasp when I saw the sender. Page 45, the comic book shop. You must have pre-ordered it before your death. I stood there clutching it to my chest thinking about what would be inside. It was like holding a piece of you.

I carefully opened it and slid it out of the envelope. It is what I had hoped it would be, but also what I feared it was. The *Locke and Key/Sandman* crossover comic. Issue Two. We had both been so excited about this series—two of our favourite comics joining forces to make one super comic. We talked about it for months, piecing together any crumbs of information that we stumbled upon. Speculating about this comic was one of our favourite pastimes. Issue One left us both reeling. How could we possibly wait for Issue Two?

I remember when we knew you were dying and they told us you had months to live you kept saying, "Please let me live to see Issue Two. I have to know what happens." It was only a month away. Surely you would make it and get to see what happened next. But you didn't.

I tried to recreate the experience of sharing a new comic with you. I always let you read it first and watched you as you read it internally with only the sound of the pages turning to give me a clue about the content. Then you would close it up and tell me to "Buckle up" and I knew the story would be a great one. Then it was your turn to watch me as I read it externally making all sorts of noises and gasping and shouting at the page (occasionally falling off the sofa or having to get up and run around in a circle if things were extremely exciting) and then the bliss of being able to talk about it. For hours. And begin our speculation about the next issue.

Oh Thomas, this issue was a cracker! I fell off the sofa on the first page and it only got better from there. But at the end there was no one to talk to and my heart felt like a stone in my chest. It was the first time I understood the expression "my heart grew heavy." It just sat in my chest getting heavier and heavier until it dropped into the pit of my stomach.

Here is where our lives diverge—I carry on and you are perpetuating stuck on Issue One.

All my love,
Heather

21/04/2021

Dear Best Beloved,

It has been five weeks today since you left me. I thought I had been doing so well. I have been practical. I have been organised. I have filled out reams of paperwork. We both know that paperwork is not my strong suit. Anxiety makes the words morph and change on the page to say something else entirely. How many times did I rush to you in panic thinking an official letter was asking one thing (a terrible, difficult thing) when really it was asking a relatively easy thing? We used to laugh at the way my brain played tricks on me. So now, without you, I must read and re-read and read aloud over several days to be sure I am reading it correctly.

I thought I was doing so well. But these last few days have been extremely hard emotionally. I feel like I am falling apart—that bits of my heart are just crumbling away leaving me empty inside. The whole house seems to be copying my emotional state. The boiler packed up twice in seven days leaving me without hot water. The plug sockets in the kitchen both stopped working. The one on the right hasn't worked since we moved in seven years ago, but now the one on the left has gone too. I had to run the blender in the living room. Lightbulbs flicker whenever I enter the room. The cordless phone has a light that blinks but when I press the button it says there are no messages. The laptop freezes and my phone continually restarts itself without me asking it to.

At one point I hoped that maybe you were trying to send me a message like in *Stranger Things* where Will who was taken to the Upside Down communicated with his mother through the Christmas lights. But I suspect that my high levels of anxiety and grief are increasing my electromagnetic field.

But I desperately want a message from you. I don't care if it caused everything to go wrong and the house was plunged into darkness and the water came out of the taps frozen and nothing worked. If I could hear you, if I could see you again and feel your strong arms wrapped around me, I would gladly endure it because anything is better than this grief.

All my love,
Heather

26/04/2021

Dear Best Beloved,

I found it. A message from you. I saw that our favourite shop Skelton Crew who makes all the Locke and Key merch was selling the Key to Hell from the Locke and Key/Sandman crossover comic. Here is something that can bridge our two lives together, with you in the past and me in the future. If you were alive I know we would have ordered it to add to our key collection. I sat there by the computer terrified because I have only just mastered ordering online from Argos and this website was different. Eventually I figured it out (after a bit of sweat and tears, but thankfully no blood) and it will be winging its way across the ocean to me. To us.

The key was just the key I was searching for. In the comics, John Locke has put himself into Hell out of guilt and shame for his actions. His sister Mary has gone to rescue him because he has punished himself enough and deserves forgiveness. I have felt scorched by the Hell that is being alive when you are not, but as we know keys turn both ways. I can lock myself in a prison of despair or I can use it to open my shackles and keep up with the things we both loved to keep your memory alive. So, let me continue to curate the collection and keep you close to me.

All my love,
Heather

27/04/2021

Dear Best Beloved,

I posted some of your ashes to the United States today. I had been practicing for this moment for weeks. I had researched the legalities of sending human ashes through the post: Royal Mail allows no more than fifty grams, and they must be in a sift-proof container in a well-secured and cushioned envelope. The sender's name and address must be clearly visible on the front and the customs label must declare that contained within are the remains of a person or animal. It also must be sent tracked and signed for.

I did a trial run weeks ago speaking to a postal worker for advice. Does the fifty grams include the weight of the envelope? No one had ever asked her that before so she recommended that I put in forty grams as the envelope would weigh ten grams. She was so kind—she was also a widow—and she gave me the customs forms to fill out at home so I wouldn't cry trying to write them on the spot.

I packaged you up carefully, weighing you on my kitchen scale to be sure you were no more than the required weight. In the morning I tried the eyeliner trick. I have found if I wear eyeliner, I can stop myself from sobbing unexpectedly in public by telling myself that my makeup will run. This is usually enough to keep the tears at a modest trickle rather than a flood. But not today. The act of explaining the contents of the envelopes to the startled postal employee and then handing over a print-out from the Royal Mail website to show I had done my research and him going down the checklist to see if I had packaged you correctly was too much to bear. I started to cry—properly wail—and could not stop the haunted keening that erupted from deep within my belly. I snotted in my mask.

After that I had to get through the posting of six additional items. In retrospect I should have saved you for last. It took longer than I expected, and I had to go straight to work. I arrived looking like a sad panda. But it is done. You are winging your way back to the place of your birth. I like the idea of you being remembered in so many places, but it was terribly difficult to let you go.

All my love,
Heather

28/04/2021

Dear Best Beloved,

It has been six weeks since you left this world. Sometimes I feel like I am losing touch with you. I have had nightmares where I feel panicked because I cannot recognise you anymore.

We never were the sort who kept pictures of ourselves around the house. Why would we? We didn't need photographs because we had each other. I loved the way your face would light up when you saw me. My heart never failed to flutter in my chest when I heard your key in the door and your voice calling my name. I would leap up and throw my arms around you and then look into your eyes as you looked into mine and feel the deepest gratitude that you had come home to me. Now no one comes home to me.

I decided what I needed was photographs. If I could see you everywhere I looked then I could find your face in my dreams. So, I went to Boots the Chemist and printed off five of my favourite photos—two of us together in healthier, happier times and three of you. I went to Wilkos and bought frames and spent the evening putting them all together. I shall put you in every room so that I have someone to talk to.

I find it a bit hard to look at the photos at the moment as I had forgotten how beautiful you were. It makes my throat ache to look at you and know that in this lifetime you will never again come through the door and call my name. But it will get easier to look upon you and someday I will be able to see you and remember with a smile and not tears.

That's the theory, anyway.

All my love,
Heather

Dear Best Beloved,

One of the things I loved about you was that you were a collector and an organiser. It all stems from being a librarian, I think. You were also a procrastinator.

One of the collections you cultivated over the years was the first thirty years of *Cricket Magazine* for children. It started with the copies that had been owned by your sister and handed down to you. Then you searched Ebay and did some bartering and wheeling and dealing and got every single issue in the first thirty years. You were always so good at finding bargains.

For over a decade you had been saying you wanted to create an index for the first thirty years of *Cricket*. It would be a splendid index divided by subject, title, author, and table of contents. It would be a labour of love that you would present to the team at *Cricket Magazine* because there wasn't a proper index. You knew this because you tried to buy a copy from them, and they lamented that there wasn't one.

In typical Thomas fashion you bought ring binders, paper, colour coded subject dividers, designed intricate cover art using the characters Cricket and Ladybug from the magazine and then never actually did any indexing.

About once a year you would take the binders out of the drawers and get the first issue of *Cricket* and start to take notes, but then the crease would appear between your eyebrows as you clicked the pen on your teeth.

"I just need to think how to approach this properly," you would say, and all the indexes would go back in the drawers.

I really wanted the drawer space but did not want to get rid of the four unfinished index binders because even a failed index is a part of who you were—passionate about children's literature but also glacially slow at deciding how to do something "just right."

I discovered that if I stacked up the four binders, they were the perfect height for a footstool to help me sit comfortably at my new computer chair. This gave me an idea. I wrapped them with a thick piece of elastic to keep them from sliding and inserted a yoga cushion on top. Then I sewed a little pillowcase from an old duvet cover with the poppers on the end so I could slide the books inside.

Now I have a beautiful just-the-right-height footstool to go with my just-right office chair. I have a piece of you resting under my feet as I type at the computer and craft stories.

And I finally have my drawers back.

All my love,
Heather

MAY

02/05/2021

Dear Best Beloved,

I have suffered a storytelling related injury. This is not so unusual as I tend to bruise easily. You used to look at my shins in horror and ask, "How did you do that? What did you run into?" and I would always shrug my shoulders because I had no idea. It could be one of many things that I had crashed into over the past few days. But this one I know.

Yesterday between customers I was practicing *Horton Hears a Who* by Dr Seuss to be filmed for the bookshop's YouTube channel. It is a story that requires me to go down on one knee several times and I usually get a small bruise from doing it but somehow yesterday I came down on it wrong and today I have a whopping great purple bruise shaped a bit like a flying dragon surrounded by lots of smaller yellow bruises (which are from prior acts of clumsiness). I went to the shop today to film it and I was worried about having to kneel repeatedly on it as it is very tender. So, I stuffed a wodge of polyfill stuffing into my tights around my knee. It gave me a huge puffy cushion that looked ridiculous, but the kneeling was virtually painless, and I managed to film it all on my own without you which was a big accomplishment. You would be so proud of me. Now I just need to edit it before the fifteenth of May.

All my love,
Heather

03/05/2021

Dear Best Beloved,

Feeling despondent and hopeless today. I was so proud of myself. I was determined to get back to storytelling. I was determined to prove I could film myself telling a tale for the bookshop's YouTube channel without your help. That I could do it on my own. But I am no good without you.

For thirty-two years we have been a team. Ever since we were at college I was in the spotlight, and you were my backstage crew. You were my stage manager, my light and sound man, my photographer, and my problem solver. You were always there making everything run smoothly.

I filmed it yesterday, despite my knee injury. I tried very hard to be both you and me. I carried the table downstairs by myself and set up the camera precariously balancing my tripod on a stack of books. The tripod kept falling and once the table collapsed and had to be repositioned. That alone took nearly an hour then I had to keep filming test shots to see if I was in the frame. How I longed for you to be there to adjust the camera while I stood there on my mark. I had to film it twice because the first time I didn't notice that the tripod holding the phone was in shot. Exhausted, I tried again knowing that it was the best day to film because it was my day off. It can't be done when the shop is open, and it can't be done on a day that I have worked as my chronic pain will not allow it. My body is just not capable of it.

I was so happy. I just kept imagining you smiling down on me telling me you were so proud of me for figuring it out.

But I didn't, did I Best Beloved? I screwed it up. When I went to upload it to the computer tonight, I realised that I had filmed it wrong It needed to be landscape and not portrait. How could I not remember how you did it? I was just crushed that it took me three times as long and I still didn't do it right.

Why aren't you here to help me? I am no good without you, Thomas. I need you. I want you back. I want you here. I want to do this with you and not on my own. I can't act without my trusty cameraman. Why did you have to leave me? There was so much more joy when we did it together.

But I will just have to do it again, learn from my mistakes and carry on. But I don't want to. Not without you.

All my love,
Heather

04/05/2021

Dear Best Beloved,

I finally dreamed of you last night, but it was not the dream I was hoping for.

In my dream our refrigerator was leaking. There was water everywhere. It was pouring like a tidal wave from beneath the door. I called for you to come and help, but you did not come. I screamed your name over and over until my throat was raw and finally you appeared lazily strolling around the corner. I barked orders to move my library books which were in a paper bag perilously close to the floodgate while I went to go grab towels to sop up the mess. I came racing back clutching every towel we owned, and you were still there, standing just as you had before, looking on disinterested as my library books were washed down the stairs. Suddenly the fury that I felt came racing through the dry husk of my body and set me alight. I could see into my chest cavity and my heart was a smouldering tumbleweed that rolled out of my body and crashed into you causing you to spontaneously combust. All that was left of you was a pile of ash. I sank down into the rising water and realised it was not our refrigerator that was leaking but my eyes. All the flood waters were tears, and I was going to drown.

I woke up with my heart drumming in my chest and the feeling of being both shivering cold and wet and dry like scorched grass in a drought. I felt abandoned by you when I needed you most. And I know that you didn't want to leave me, and I know that you only left because you had no choice, but it hurts. And I don't know how I am going to get through it.

All my love,
Heather

05/05/2021

Dear Best Beloved,

It is seven weeks today since you left me. I don't seem to be doing that well. I find that I am crying a rainstorm of tears. I feel like a worn-out old shirt hung out on the clothesline that keeps getting caught in the cycle of a deluge and then squeezed through the mangle. Then the heat of the sun blisters me until I am threadbare and the whole thing starts all over again. I find myself having to retreat into the cupboard under the stairs at work to cry it out between customers more and more.

So, tonight I tried to work on something positive. We had so many lovely cards and letters from caring people before and after you died that I thought they needed a proper home. I decided to wrap up a shoebox to make it nicer. It took me three goes to get the paper neat, but I finally did it. You would have gotten it in one as you were always better at wrapping presents than me. I used brown paper because we had some and I know you would have felt it was a wasteful extravagance to buy a roll of wrapping paper.

"Where will you keep it? What will you do with the rest of it?" I heard you ask, and you'd be right, so brown paper it is.

It looked so plain, and I wanted to put something special on top, so I used a photo of an Atlas Moth. I have fond memories of a row of chrysalis hanging from our shower rail that you brought home from your weekend job at the Botanic Gardens. Life with you was never dull. We waited weeks but finally managed to hatch eight Atlas Moths who flew around our house until they died. I was worried about food, but you told me they don't have mouths as their time on Earth is so short that they don't waste it eating. They just look to find a mate and then die. They were beautiful and sad so I thought they would be perfect.

I can't look at the cards and letters again. Not yet. I am too fragile. Just putting them in the box caused a tidal wave of tears. But someday I hope I will be able to look back on their love and it will bring me comfort.

But not yet.

All my love,
Heather

06/05/2021

Dear Best Beloved,

It was election day. A big one—three ballots. My first election voting without you. I wasn't even sure I was going to be able to do it because I wasn't quite sure where our polling station is. You were always my compass, my map reader, my sense of direction. You used to joke that my sense of direction was so poor that I couldn't find my own butt with a map and a torch. Even if there was a big neon sign that said YOUR BUTT in ten-foot-high letters and an arrow pointing to my own backside there was still a chance I might get lost. You were only mildly exaggerating.

But I woke up today and knew I had to do it. We fought very hard to become citizens of this great nation. We paid exorbitant fees and took a written test so that we could have the privilege of voting. I got up early and headed in the direction of the polling station. That much I knew. Which way to go. But how far or the name of the street eluded me. I was always such a following sheep with you. I let you play the shepherd and I happily followed trotting beside you on my dachshund legs as you took your seven-league-boots steps. The curse of being a short-arse married to a tall man.

The one thing I did remember was that the polling station was down a street with a church, and the church had a Weeping Angel in the graveyard (the scary *Doctor Who* kind not the sad crying kind). Armed in the knowledge that I was looking for a church, I peered down every side street until I saw the towering spire. Suddenly it looked familiar and so I confidently made my way towards the church (and the scary angel) and went into the church hall.

I went in and said my name. I took a deep breath and asked for them to check if you had been taken off the register. You had. I found that both comforting that it had been done as paperwork takes ages and terribly sad as here was one more way you had been wiped from existence. They were sorry for my loss.

I stood there in the study carrel with my stubby pencil putting my X on the bits of paper before posting them through the plastic tub with the slit on top. Do you remember how much we laughed the first time we voted in the United Kingdom? It was all so low tech. Pencil. Paper. Little divided cubicles to keep your neighbour from cheating off your test. It was like voting for Prom Queen you said.

I finished and as I walked out the door into the warm sunlight another tidal wave of emotion washed over me. I cried all the way home. Some from the relief of having found the polling station on my own and some for knowing that you will never vote again.

Just another way that I will have to go on without you.

All my love,
Heather

11/05/2021

Dear Best Beloved,

I let the landline go today. I never really used it since I got my mobile phone. It was you—my Best Beloved luddite—who insisted we have one since you refused to have a mobile phone. We needed it, you said, to call family in the United States. But we didn't, not really. These days I use Messenger or WhatsApp. And I was the one doing the calling anyway. You hated to talk on the phone.

It feels like giving a piece of you away. That you were somehow part of the old-fashioned phone. If you could have found a rotary phone you probably would have bought it.

If you had recorded the message on the answerphone, I would have saved it forever because I don't have a recording of your voice. By the time we thought of it, you couldn't speak anymore. But it never would have been you who recorded the message, would it? It was always me who had to do those sorts of things. What I wouldn't give to hear your soft-spoken drawl again.

It had to be done. I need to pare back my outgoings quite severely. Even though you have left me with pensions and life insurance, it is only enough to live on for a decade and I suspect that I have a long way to go before I see you again. If you had died when we were old and grey like we planned the wait would not be so long and the money would have lasted me.

Probate is costing me two month's salary and I need every penny I can get, so the landline had to go. I phoned British Telecom (another of your jobs that I am now forced to do) and renegotiated our contract. My contract. BT took off £22 a month and reduced my Broadband package to a manageable figure when I cried and explained why I didn't need the landline. I said it was yours and you are absent from this life, and I cannot afford such luxuries anymore. They were kind.

And so, it is done. I am a one-phone household. A one-person household. Singular and alone.

All my love,
Heather

12/05/2021

Dear Best Beloved,

It's eight weeks since you left me. Two months. I am in a permanent state of aching. My head and my heart pound to the same rhythm of He's GONE. He's GONE. He's GONE. In my throat there is a stone that chokes me when I try to speak and a tightness in my perpetually clenched jaw. My throat feels raw and my voice—husky and hoarse—has a way of doubling back on itself when I try to speak. I must swallow my words to hold back the tide of emotion I carry around within me.

Everyone says, "Go ahead and cry. It's alright to let it go." But they have no idea what they are asking for. They watch me as my eyes brim with tears. They see the solitary tear trickle down my cheek. They think that is what they are encouraging me to do. But that is not what lurks inside me. My heart is a tidal wave, a tsunami of grief that will flood the whole of my body and come vomiting out my mouth with a heart-breaking wail. If I stop clenching my jaw or open my mouth wide enough to speak without swallowing it back it will erupt like Vesuvius, and I will explode.

"But you need to cry," I hear people say. But I also must live in this world. So, I tighten my body and forcibly stuff it down to stop it from happening because once it starts it can take hours to stop. I cannot be like that at work. I cannot work a five-hour shift sitting on the floor, pulling my hair, boiling over with snot because I need this job. I am the breadwinner now. I have to make ends meet. And so, to all the well-meaning people who tell me to "let it flow"—they can all go to Hell and stop telling me what to do because they have no clue.

All my love,
Heather

15/05/2021

Dear Best Beloved,

It's the fifteenth of May and you know what happened on the fifteenth of May, don't you? Of course you do. How could you forget?

On this day, the fifteenth of May, in the heat of the day and the cool of the pool deep within the Jungle of Nool, that all important event occurred: Horton heard a Who. This was the first story that I ever memorised. I have been telling this tale since the age of sixteen and you, like me, loved it and celebrated the fifteenth of May as it if were a holiday. We would spend the day quoting the book to each other.

That is why it was so important to have the storytelling video ready for today. I chose this story especially because I already knew all the words. My brain is struggling to think and retain—my head is full of cotton wool since your untimely death—and I thought it would be wise to get back into storytelling gently. Unfortunately, the first time didn't go as well as I had planned, and I came home feeling so afraid that this huge part of my life—weaving tales and spinning stories—would be over without you. Because who can I ask to help with this? Who would give up several hours on a Sunday, patiently help and watch and listen and prompt me with a line when needed or calm me down if I flubbed that line for the third time? Who would know just the right thing to make a second take even better than the first? Who but you would do it gladly and lovingly? Nobody, that's who. Nobody will ever love me the way that you do.

And so, I knew if this was going to happen, I had to put on my "big girl panties" and try again. I have long held the opinion that people will only let me down and if I want something done right, I have to do it myself. Or ask you. You were a person of your word.

I went back the following weekend and the setting up went much quicker and I positioned the camera correctly and I got it in one take and went home. And so here it is, the fifteenth of May and I have a story to tell. I am trying (and often failing) to build resilience. I hope you are proud of that.

All my love,
Heather

20/05/2021

Dear Best Beloved,

Someone said to me today, "It's no wonder you are in shock and crying in the cupboards at work. Y'all didn't have much time between the time you found that he had terminal cancer and his death. How much time are we talking about—three and a half, four months?"

No. It was just over six weeks. Forty-five days. Nineteen of those days you were in hospital away from me. I remember being weirdly grateful that you started everything on the first of the month as it made the maths easier. You went into hospital on the first of February. We saw the Oncologist on the first of March. You died on Saint Patrick's Day, seventeen days later.

Twenty-eight days in February and seventeen in March were all we had to prepare.

It truly is the devil's arithmetic where $28 + 17 = 0$.

All my love,
Heather

21/05/2021

Dear Best Beloved,

We never liked to be apart, did we? We always said we were conjoined souls who could not bear to be separated. We have a friend whose wife travels for work and was gone for weeks at a time. We have a friend who was in the military and spent five years away from his family doing tours of duty in Iraq. We thanked God every day that this was not our life because we both said we could not endure it. And here I am having to endure it.

In nearly twenty-nine years of marriage, we were only separated overnight sixty-five times.

Eight days when you were in the hospital in 1996 being diagnosed with cancer.

Ten days when I chaperoned a trip of high school students in Europe with my mother.

Seven days when I was in hospital in 2010 having the horrible hysterectomy.

Two days when you went to Wales to interview for a job while I stayed in England.

Sixteen days when I went back the United States to see family.

Three days when I went on a girlie holiday with a friend to London.

Nineteen days when you were in the hospital before you died.

Today I have been without you as many days as we had been separated in our entire married life together. But there will be no sweet reunion this time. No hearing you call my name and whistling our secret tune that meant "I love you'" as you walked through the door. There will be no bounding into your arms like Tigger. There is just nothingness as I come home to an empty house with the shadows that you left behind.

All my love,
Heather

28/05/2021

Dear Best Beloved,

I had my booster jab today. I got the AstraZeneca again. I got the first one in March because they wanted me to be able to protect you from Covid. In the end you didn't need it because you died three days later. It made me feel awful—achy with chills like a bad case of the flu. I hate that in your last days I was feeling so rough. I worried that I wasn't taking care of you properly. As if you would let me take care of you. You were a terrible patient; you always were.

I keep thinking about the article I read in *The Guardian* about how occasionally someone who had the AstraZeneca would get a blood clot and die. I am ashamed to say I have been wishing for it to happen. I have been feeling every beat of my heart, every pulse, and willing it to clog, to clot, to thicken up and break off and sail through my bloodstream straight to my heart so I can fly to meet you on the Other Side. I am frightened and repelled by this thought and yet, it comes back again and again. I wonder if I should tell someone, but I am too ashamed to say anything.

Sometimes as I am crossing the road, I think about being in that song by The Smiths and imagining a double decker bus crashing into me. It wouldn't be suicide, you see. it would be an accident. An accident that would let me die by your side, such a heavenly way to die. I would never walk out into traffic, but I do sometimes day-dream about being in an accident which would be no fault of my own. But I know I can't tell anyone these things because they will think I am mad and worry about me. I don't have anyone to tell but you.

I find myself hoping that I will just go to sleep and not wake up but I have not been granted the *liberty to die* (as Emily Dickinson says) because every morning I am still alive. My first thoughts are often a crushing disappointment that I am still here and then I am flooded with hot shame like lava for rejecting this gift of life that I have been given.

I won't act on any of this. They are just thoughts. I know you would want me to continue to "Be the light" and so I shall though I do feel much dimmer without you.

All my love,
Heather

JUNE

05/06/2021

Dear Best Beloved,

Today is our anniversary. It still is even though you are not here with me to celebrate. It would have been our twenty-ninth year of marriage. I must use the conditional tense "would have been" because you didn't live to see it. Next year I will have to refer to this day in the past tense and say, "We were married for nearly twenty-nine years."

When they told us that you had months to live, we thought we would have one last anniversary together. One last time to celebrate the joy that has been our marriage. But instead, you had weeks, and we spent those last days writing a hasty will and making sure that my name was listed as beneficiary on all the important papers before you lost the ability to think and speak or sign your name.

I have been doing alright. Just alright. It still feels as though I have been flayed alive—my skin peeled from my muscles and my bones crushed by the weight of grief. But yesterday I felt so overwhelmed at the thought of today that I wept until I was limp and swollen from the salt in my tears.

I struggled to wake up today. I wanted so badly to dream of you. I kept pressing the snooze alarm hoping I would see you, feel you, know that were close, but I had nothing but a dreamless sleep. A void. I finally roused myself and threw on some clothes and left for work, dishevelled and puffy-eyed.

Every Friday the lovely vegan ice cream van comes to town, and so yesterday I went to buy a scoop before I went to work. I sobbed the whole way there, cried when I tried to place my order and my visible distress caused the kind owner to give me my cone for free. I sat in the hot sun licking my scoop of mint chocolate chip—your favourite—as the tears trickled down my face and the ice cream melted and dripped down my wrist leaving me a soggy, sticky mess. Then I went to work.

I worked upstairs today shelving books as long as I could as I just didn't feel like I could face customers. A friend stopped by and brought me a vegan chocolate shake which made me cry again (I seem to spend my days either about to cry, sobbing or recovering from crying) and the sugar helped give me energy to face the rest of the day. I tried to think what I would do when I came home. I am trying to celebrate, but I don't feel like there is any joy in it without you.

Many people have said I should do what we would have done together in memory of you. But it is not the same without you. Nothing is the same without you. But I will try. I am so thankful that we had each other. You were such a wonderful husband, partner, friend, lover, mischief-maker, smarty-pants and compassionate beardy-weirdy and I am so glad that you were mine. Happy anniversary my Best Beloved.

All my love,
Heather

Dear Best Beloved,

Today is my day of rest, my day off after a very long week at work. I decided to spend the day looking back at happier times.

Our wedding was the most beautiful wedding there has ever been. I know everyone thinks that, but in our case it was true. We did everything our way despite what convention dictated and it was such a wonderful joyous occasion.

We had so much fun writing the whole ceremony ourselves. I loved the way we based it on Medieval traditions and wore silvery pink clothes which would have been at home at a Renaissance Faire. We didn't like the concept of my father "giving away" his daughter to her husband as if I was a piece of property to be transferred between men so we chose a church with two aisles instead of a centre aisle so that your parents could walk you down one aisle and my parents could walk me down the other. Instead of a traditional wedding march we picked Beethoven's *Für Elise*—a song I fell in love with in the eighth grade when a friend played it for me on her piano. We had readings from Thomas Malory's *Le Morte d'Arthur* and I sang a ballad by Smithfield Fair acapella that talked about how far and long I would travel to bring you home again to me. I sang this song to you as you were dying, and you took your last breath on the last note. Such a tender beginning and end. You recited Shakespeare sonnet 29 (*"For thy sweet love remembered such wealth brings/That then I scorn to change my state with kings."*)

Every year on our anniversary we always listened to *Für Elise* and renewed our vows: *From this day forward, I am committing myself to you in marriage. I promise to love, respect, and trust you; to teach you and learn from you; to celebrate and grieve with you; and to be true and loyal to you as long as I shall live.*

The reception was a triumph with a dark chocolate cake covered with white chocolate frosting and a string quartet. Our flowerless flower girl who wore jingle bells on her wrists and skipped down the aisle also played *Greensleeves* on the harp. The food was delicious and so many lovely people came. We had so much fun and were the last people to leave. This was very unusual for a wedding as usually the bride and groom rush away after they have had a bit of cake, but we wanted to enjoy it. To savour it. To soak up every ounce of joy there was and bring it with us as we began a life as husband and wife. It was a magical night followed by a "staycation" honeymoon where we went to City Park Players and saw *Come Back to the Five and Dime, Jimmy Dean, Jimmy Dean* and to the Dollar Cinema to see *Fried Green Tomatoes* and the mall to buy our first set of bookshelves. It was just the sort of life we wanted with books and adventures and the theatre.

I miss you T. No one can compare to you. Thank you for loving me.

All my love,
Heather

Dear Best Beloved,

It has been three months since you died. Twelve weeks Eighty-five days. I feel like I have aged decades since I last held your hand, but in truth I still have decades left to go before we meet again. It is hard taking the slow road.

My life has changed so much in the last few months. Not just the emptiness of the house or the lack of affection or the reality that I probably will never have sex again but the fact that I am in charge of doing everything on my own.

Thomas, you were always so supportive. When I needed a better work-life balance to deal with my chronic pain you gave me the gift of only working part-time and you worked longer hours (or took a second job) to make sure I didn't have to. Now I am the bread-winner. You took up the slack when I needed a break and now, I just have to get on with it without someone to help. And so, I have had to figure out ways to help me do the things you used to do. Many were gifts from kind friends, and I am grateful for each one. I named them all just like we named the bookshelves and thinking of obscure names made me laugh at how you would have immediately under-stood where my idea came from. You always got my references.

First, my shopping trolley Mina Murray which was a gift from Sage. You used to joke you were my "pack mule" and I only married you so you would carry the heavy stuff. I don't have a strong man to carry home all my groceries anymore, but Mina helps me remain independent. She actually can carry more than you. But I would trade her to have you back again.

Second, Zeppelin my ladder which was a gift from my bosses Ash and Rea. I am a short-arse and you loved doing all the high up jobs for me. But I have no tall man in my life anymore. But thankfully I can reach everything I need with this step ladder. But I would trade it in a heartbeat to be able to nestle under your arm like a bird under your wing.

Third, my air fryer named Stephen Fryer which was a gift from Dawn. Cooking for one is so much harder. I used to enjoy planning meals that I knew you would love and watching your face light up at the taste of my cooking. Now no one is excited to eat my food. This air fryer makes it much easier and quicker to make a meal for one. But I would give anything to hear you exclaim, "Yum! My favourite!" like you did about everything I made.

Fourth, one I bought myself. It is a red stool named Hester Prynne. My job requires standing on my feet for hours without getting to sit down. The last thing I need when I come home is to have to stand up in the kitchen while I try to prepare and cook something healthy. Sometimes I come home and the pain in my back is so bad that all I can do is have a lie down. On those days you used to let me rest while you cooked. In fact, we made a new year's resolution that you would cook more to allow me to rest, but now I must fend for myself. Hester means I can take the weight off my feet and rest while I try to cobble something healthy together. But I would endure the most agonising pain if I could cook for you again.

The fifth one I also bought myself and the kind-hearted owner Paul from my favourite tea shop in town drove me out to the office supply store to buy it and then carried it up the stairs into the living room. It is a proper office chair—also red—to use when I am working at the computer whom I have named Ionesco. This chair makes my back pain bearable so that I can write stories and do video editing, but I would gladly sit on the rickety chair (or the "wickety chair" as you would have called it in your best Rik Mayall voice) if it would bring you back.

Lastly, little Tom Dacre, the carpet sweeper. I bought this for myself because the hoover is too heavy to schlep up and down the stairs in our split-level home. I could never do it myself and had to ask you to bring it from room to room so I could vacuum the carpet and each time afterwards, I would have to lie down from the pain of pushing our extremely heavy and awkward appliance around. Let's be honest, you didn't marry me for my housekeeping skills. But with little Tom Dacre there is much more of a chance that I won't be living in a rubbish heap. But I would clean every surface on my hands and knees until it sparkled if I could scrub away your death and resurrect you with a yellow duster cloth.

So, you see Best Beloved, I am getting on. I am figuring out how to replace you. But you can't really be replaced and so I must make do. What choice do I have?

All my love,
Heather

16/06/2021

Dear Best Beloved,

Today is the day that the winners of the Carnegie and Greenaway awards were announced. I had forgotten, only nudged to remember because I saw it on Twitter. You wouldn't have forgotten. You never forgot. You knew the dates of all the book awards. If we were apart for the day, you would excitedly email me. But you weren't here to remind me this year, Best Beloved.

The Carnegie and Greenaway awards hold extra importance for us as they are awards for best children's/young adult novel and best illustrated picture book. One of the things that I loved about you was your passion and breadth of knowledge about children's books. I tried to rival you, but you were the master.

For the last several years as soon as the longlist was published, we would head to the library and order every book they had and try to read them all—endlessly discussing their merits—as we tried to predict the shortlist and ultimately the winners. In 2017 for our silver wedding anniversary, you won us tickets to the awards in a charity auction and we got to be there and see if our chosen winners were successful. We were able to meet all the authors and illustrators that were nominated, and that year Lane Smith won the Greenaway Award, and we were so excited. He couldn't quite believe it when we pulled out our twenty-year-old copies of *The Stinky Cheese Man*, *Math Curse* and *Squids Will Be Squids* for him to sign.

In 2020 we didn't get to do our annual tradition because the library was closed for so many months due to the pandemic, but something better happened—after five years of trying you were selected to be a judge for the Carnegie and Greenaway Awards in 2022. When the news came through that your application had been successful it was one of the happiest moments in our life. I was so proud of you. The expression "bursting with pride" was so true—it was like my heart grew three sizes just thinking about how exciting this was going to be. Hundreds of free books—quality children's books—would arrive on our doorstep. We would read and discuss and ponder and debate and take notes and talk late into the night and compare and contrast and it was going to be so much fun. A real bucket list activity with you as a judge and me as a secret shadow judge. We had plans to donate the books to schools and the library and friends when it was all over. It was going to be wonderful.

Then you went into hospital. Those agonising nineteen days where we didn't know what was happening, only the word, the terrible word, CANCER which struck us both with such fear. When you left the hospital, we were told that you would be seeing an Oncologist and that you would be starting chemotherapy. This was when we still had hope—when we thought it would just be another fight. That we had beaten it before, and we could beat it again. I remember how you cried because you recalled how painful, how debilitating chemo had been for you in 1996. After much discussion you contacted the committee and explained that your upcoming chemotherapy would most likely mean that you would not have the energy or focus to complete your duties. I recall how small you looked, my big strong mountain of a man. The grief of having to let go of it made you shrink. They were kind and understanding and offered you a place in 2023 if you wanted it. You wanted it very much. I wanted it very much.

Three weeks later you were dead. What we thought was going to be a terrible year but then it would get better turned into the unthinkable. The worst year that will never get better because you are not here to share it with me.

I didn't know the books that won, but I will seek them out. But I have no one to share them with. And that Best Beloved, is the cruellest trick of all.

All my love,
Heather

27/06/2021

Dear Best Beloved,

It is my un-birthday today. As a child who had a mother born on the 26th of June and a father born on the 28th of June, a small girl with a December birthday felt very left out and so it was decreed that the day in between their birthdays should be my un-birthday. And so it has been since I was a tiny child.

I still celebrate it. Because why wouldn't I? You used to tease me every year making a big song and dance about how an un-birthday is not a real birthday and was just a con to get presents. But you always bought me a gift, Best Beloved. And a good one. Nobody could beat you on the gift-giving front.

So, it seemed a good day to finally lay you to rest. This year I am giving you the gift of a forever home beneath the shady trees where sheep may safely graze.

I had been waiting for a Sunday where the weather was good. Today was sunny, but not too hot. Perfect. I packed your biodegradable urn made from handmade paper imprinted with flowers into my trusty shopping trolley and went to catch the train.

Here was the first hiccup. The train was cancelled, and I nearly cried when I heard the dreaded words "replacement bus service." Then I did cry when the driver awkwardly manhandled my trolley onto the minibus and tried to shove it sideways. I had to explain about my precious cargo and the worry that a bumpy ride down winding Welsh roads might dislodge your ashes. The driver helped me to remove the urn which I carried on my lap and cried until my mask was damp with sweat and tears.

A young mum and her small boy were sitting behind me, and I could hear her son who was desperate to give me a hug "to make that sad lady feel better." His mother explained that he couldn't hug me right now but maybe he could give me something special to cheer me up. A small and sticky hand presented me with a pinecone he had found (the best one, he told me) and I have taken it home and put it on the dresser next to your wooden pot of ashes. I will treasure it.

Then as the bus wound its way to Whitland what should come on the radio but *Domino* by Jessie J. Do you remember that holiday we stayed in the windmill in Dunstable, Best Beloved? Every night as we cooked supper side by side *Domino* came on the radio and we would sing along and dance in the kitchen. I always associate that song with happiness and holidays.

I arrived and they met me at the station. We had a lovely outdoor lunch of fresh salad and homemade hummus and the bread I had baked that morning then we set about with the task at hand.

We wheeled you out in the wagon they use to carry sacks of poo out to the big pile beyond the trees (now renamed the Pitchford Pile in your honour since you volunteered so lovingly each week picking up animal poo to allow them to get on with animal care) while I played *Für Elise* from my phone. They had even decorated the wagon with some spider bunting for the occasion which made me laugh.

We dug you a little hole and hung some small stone cherubs in the nearby trees. We said our goodbyes, I sang the song I sang at our wedding—the song I sang as you died in my arms. We laughed and decided to scoop in a bit of sheep poo in there with you and then we covered you up with dirt whilst saying, "Ashes to ashes, funk to funky. We know Major Tom's a junkie."

We found a perfect slate to be a marker for you and perhaps I will return in a few weeks, paint pot in hand, to write on there a message of love. A eulogy to the man you were. Though no slate would be big enough to encompass all that you were—all that you still are to me.

All my love to you, my Best Beloved, my Amazing Spiderman, my soulmate.
Heather

30/06/2021

Dear Best Beloved,

I came across a little note from you today written on a scrap of paper I found wedged in the back of a drawer. It wasn't a note of consequence. It just said that you loved me and don't forget to pick up "banjos" on my way home. It made me smile because "banjos" was our code word for bananas after you couldn't read my writing on a shopping list.

But the thing that struck me was your signature. You had used your initials, T.P. I had forgotten the way you made your initials look like an H. You spent days practicing (like me as a teenage girl practicing my autograph for when I was famous) so that your initials would also be my initial. Just one of those little things you used to do to show me you loved me.

All my love,
Heather

JULY

Dear Best Beloved,

I am coming to terms with talking about you with strangers. As soon as I open my mouth people have the reaction, "You're not from around here, are you?" Every day I meet people who want to know my story. They want to know how I got from Louisiana to Wales. I cannot tell this story without including you.

The story I usually tell is that at the age of twenty we came to the United Kingdom as exchange students, fell in love both with the nation and each other, got engaged and vowed to figure out how to emigrate. Then we did it and spent a glorious decade living in England and now are approaching the eighth wonderful year in Wales. I say that we came here to have an adventure, and we did. I still am.

Inevitably, the next question is about how we ended up in Wales. This is where it begins to get tricky. I always say we came here because you got a job as an archivist and librarian in charge of a specialist collection of books housed in the University library. But now I often say that you WORKED in Lampeter. This then prompts people to ask where you work now. Ah. I am caught out by the use of you in the past tense and I stumble trying to explain that you no longer need to work as you are dead. Gone. Ceased to be. No longer in this plane of existence.

Yesterday I had a customer who was American. I immediately

detected an accent, and we did the traditional dance of "What state do you hail from?" He was from Georgia with an accent as thick as molasses. He was from Abraham Baldwin Agricultural College and was in Wales researching about the connections between the Arthurian legends and agriculture. He asked me how we ended up here and I told our story as I always do. Our conversation went like this:

Him: You don't have much of an accent.

Me: (laughing) No, I never really did. After nearly eighteen years here I have a sort of hybrid American-British accent that makes people think I am Canadian.

Him: Does your husband have a pronounced accent?

Me: (smiling) Yes, he did have quite the drawl.

Him: (sarcastic jokey voice) What? He did and now he doesn't?

Me: No, he doesn't anymore because my husband died in March.

And this, Best Beloved, is where things always get awkward. Whenever this occurs (and it happens at least once a week) I want to say that when you were alive you had the loveliest soft drawl— Louisiana with a hint of Texas. That I would give anything to hear that voice again. To hear you say that you loved me or to playfully tell me to shut up if I was being annoying. But instead, the conversation always goes like this:

Them: (flustered and apologetic) Oh, I am so sorry.

Me: Me, too.

Then my eyes begin to well up, so I focus on trying to ring up the customer's purchases and not make eye contact. They also avert their gaze, pay for their purchases and leave. Often with another apology to which I reply that it is fine. They weren't to know. That I am still getting used to referring to you in the past tense. It is like Grief Grammar with verb tenses and the fact that I am now singular instead of plural as I diagram the sentence of my life. And grammar was never my strong suit, was it Best Beloved?

All my love,
Heather

07/07/2021

Dear Best Beloved,

I am trying new ways to talk about you—to use terminology that lets people know I am a widow. I swirl each one around in my mouth like fine wine and then spit them out. Nothing seems right. The taste of words like "late" do not suit me. I cannot seem to refer to you as my late husband because you were never late. In fact, you were ridiculously early to everything. It is one of the things I loved about you. My father was an early-bird, and we shared the frustration of my perpetually late (in the time sense, not the dead sense) mother who always believed she had plenty of time to run three errands during rush hour when she had to be at an appointment on the opposite side of town in twenty minutes. I loved that you thought of every possible thing that could go wrong and allowed a cushion of time to accommodate the apocalypse. We did a lot of standing outside venues in the cold and the rain waiting to be let in, but we were never late.

A customer who is a widower suggested the phrase "when he was alive" to preface any statement, but I found by saying, "When he was alive, he was a librarian" makes people confused. I see their thought process travel all over their face, their mouth like a fish out of water. I see them make the connection between alive and dead and I find it painful to contemplate that. One minute you were alive and then next you were dead. I had hoped that referring to the time when you were alive would bring me comfort, but it seems to have the opposite effect. The word alive cannot resurrect you.

Euphemisms like "passed away" feel like they are trying to soften the blow and they cannot. Mere words cannot soften the great injustice that was done by taking you so quickly and cruelly and leaving me alone.

The phrase "I lost my husband" conjures up an image of me carelessly leaving you somewhere, like an umbrella on the train. I picture you sitting forlornly in a cardboard box labelled Lost Property with a bunch of other husbands accidentally discarded by their distracted wives.

All I can say is that you DIED. There is no other word that expresses my grief except to look death in the eye and call it what it was.

All my love,
Heather

15/07/2021

Dear Best Beloved,

If we were still living in the United States, I think the use of you in the past tense would be a clue that you had died and people would stop probing, but here where our lives have always been a source of fascination to people, they carry on asking despite a path of clues dropped like crumbs.

The moment we ever opened our mouths, Best Beloved, people wanted to hear our story. They always want to understand how we came from Louisiana to the United Kingdom. I have to tell our story at least three times every day—and often more—each time I feel their question pick at the scab that had begun to calcify over my broken heart. All the while trying to lay out clues that we started this journey as a "we" and now there is only "me, myself and I."

People here seem to struggle to pick up on the most blatant of clues. I think perhaps because I look too young to be a widow, which I am. I am too young to have to try to forge ahead without you. They look at me and cannot fathom that this is where my story is headed. That our brave and exciting adventure has been derailed by your un-timely death. And so, they ignore the clues and probe deeper until they finally understand the reality of the situation. Then I often see them recoil as if I have "Death Cooties" which might be contagious. They realise that my jolly adventure doesn't quite have the fairy tale ending we had hoped for, and they do not know where to look or how to behave. I find myself apologising for their discomfort. How British of me.

Then the next time I open my mouth, someone else asks to hear my story. Will it ever get easier?

All my love,
Heather

23/07/2021

Dear Best Beloved,

I was having a good day. I slept without restlessness, I woke up early and exercised. I was excited to be meeting a friend for a cup of tea at Tea Traders before work. I felt the closest approximation to happiness that I had felt in months. Then I ran into an acquaintance on my way to the café who said I looked pale and drawn. She did that sympathetic head tilt which I loathe (I much prefer it if they could just look me in the eye and tell me how sorry they are for my loss) and I suddenly became self-conscious. Do I have "Resting Sad Face"? Does every person I pass by as I walk through town want to tilt their head and sigh at me? Do they look at me and see my broken heart?

All my love,
Heather

25/07/2021

Dear Best Beloved,

I cleaned the house today. Deep cleaned. Move-the-furniture sort of cleaned. It is the first time I have properly cleaned the house since you died. And it had to be done as I was drowning in clutter. Unfiled important papers dealing with your untimely demise. Post with your name on it that I couldn't bear to throw away. Little scraps of paper with notes in your microscopic handwriting that I had to decipher to see if they were important or just an expired shopping list. Multicoloured scraps of cloth and thread—so much thread—all over the floor from projects designed to keep me busy during the long and lonely hours that I spend in this house rattling around without you. Piles of books and DVDs that needed to be put back in their correct place. The DVDs date back from before you died—you had promised to do it and never got around to it. I remember being peeved as if you were being lazy and not holding up your end of the bargain, but now in hindsight it was because you were already dying, we just didn't know it yet.

I haven't been able to face the mountain of clutter without you because we used to share the chores around the house and now everything falls to me. Overwhelmed? Doesn't matter, it has to be done. Exhausted? Doesn't matter, it has to be done. Agonising back pain? Doesn't matter, it has to be done. Sobbing uncontrollably? Doesn't matter, it has to be done. Through all of this I have only had the strength to do the bare minimum. Cooking. Dishes. Laundry in the bucket with a trip to the launderette once a month to wash sheets and towels. Everything else seemed insurmountable without your help.

I loved the way we used to clean as a team. We would draw up a list of what had to be done, divide the tasks (with you taking anything that would trigger a flare up of my chronic pain), pop an 80's CD in the player and blast it while we worked. You used to say, "You start on one side, I'll start on the other and we'll meet in the middle." It was such fun to try to beat the clock by completing the list before the music ended.

It has taken me all day, from ten in the morning until ten at night. I had to rest in between heavy lifting jobs, doing yoga for the sciatica it triggered or taking a puff on my inhaler if it made it hard to breathe. But I have done it.

I will admit that it makes me feel lighter—all that clutter cleared away. Finally, a path to walk through that is not an obstacle course. But it also makes me feel heavier. Together we could have gotten in done in record time. Together we would have made it a game. We were good with games. You were the funniest person I have ever met. You could make the most mundane chore seem like a riot.

I hope that I can keep it clean, so it won't be so hard to do the next time. But it won't be as much fun. Nothing is without you.

All my love,
Heather

27/07/2021

Dear Best Beloved,

When you were dying, you left me a list of directions as to how things needed to be done. You said that this was the ONLY WAY that they could be done. I remember feeling sceptical and you scowled at me and said very firmly that you had tried other ways and they did not work, so there was no point in doing it differently. My darling stick-in-the-mud, you were so set in your ways.

I have tried to be faithful to you and log into Netflix using your system. You insisted that we had to use the tablet—the tablet that we got on sale seven years ago for cheap at Tesco and the technology was already on its way out then. The tablet takes an excruciatingly long time to warm up and so you must turn it on and plug it in about an hour before you want to watch anything to let it chug-chug-chug its way up the hill, wheezing the whole way. Then you told me to plug it in to the computer monitor to be able to watch on the big screen. Often as we watched, the tablet would hiccup and groan and stutter as it strained under the weight of streaming a film, but you told me there was no other way around it.

Well, there is. It has taken me five months to realise that I can log into Netflix on my laptop and watch it directly there. I suggested this to you once after we bought me the new laptop last January, but you told me and I quote, "You can't log into Netflix on your laptop. You can only log into Netflix through the tablet because that is what I used to set up our account."

What a load of twaddle, my darling! I wonder if you really believed that or if you got stuck in some sort of OCD cycle and felt like you had to follow a certain pattern, in a certain order. I wish you were here to ask.

You certainly did make so many things needlessly complicated. I am glad I have found a less convoluted way to do it, but I would put up with all your eccentricities if I could have you back again.

All my love,
Heather

AUGUST

01/08/2021

Dear Best Beloved,

Grief is so strange. It is always with me. Some days it lingers on my fingertips, but busy hands keep it from settling or if it does start to weigh on me, I can brush it away like crumbs. Yesterday was a good day at work. I was dressed up as Hermione from *Harry Potter* and spent the day selling books dressed in my Gryffindor costume. My favourite family of customers came with cousins in tow—everyone in fancy dress right down to the baby. We re-enacted many battles in the children's section. I could feel grief trying to settle on me like dust, but I was able to wave my wand and brush it away.

Today I cannot move for grief. Grief and fatigue weigh on me and I feel trapped under the weight of them. I could not wake up today. Even my bones cried out as if in protest. I stayed in bed most of the day, scrolling aimlessly through my phone. I feel bloated with grief, as if I have tried to swallow the memory of you and it is choking me. The crushing pain in my chest was so great at one point that I debated whether I should get out of bed to get my inhaler. I decided it wasn't asthma, just grief. There is no inhaler for grief.

Eventually I got out of bed at 3:30 and ran to Tesco before it closed at 4 p.m. What must people have thought of me in my pyjamas, bedhead, and streaming tears as I tried to fill my trolley with food in the race against the clock before they closed?

I was listening to a random 80's playlist on Spotify through my earbuds and every song reminded me of you. *Don't You Forget About Me. You Make My Dreams Come True. Holding Out for a Hero. Never Gonna Give You Up. The Power of Love. Need You Tonight. Got My Mind Set on You.* My nose started boiling over with snot so that the wet patch on my mask bloomed outward like a flower in a time lapse video as I was trying to shove money in the hand of the kindly cashier who said, "You alright, Love?" I just kept shaking my head but didn't trust myself to speak in case it should come out as a howl.

In the end I have managed to get a few things done. Two buckets of back-breaking laundry and a sink full of dishes. But I still feel off kilter, suffocating under the weight of my grief today like Giles Corey being pressed to death in Salem. I hope that I can chase it back to the perimeter of my being tomorrow.

Tomorrow is another day.

All my love,
Heather

Dear Best Beloved,

Series six of *Inside No 9* is out. How we love this anthology series. It can be funny or serious or absurd or scary, but it is consistently terrific and this one does not disappoint.

Back when you were living you were the keeper of dates. You knew the publication date or release date of everything we loved and ordered them as soon as they became available (unless they were overpriced then you kept an eagle eye on them, watching until the price fell and snagged us a bargain.)

Now I am the keeper of dates. I saw that *Inside No 9* had come out several months ago and so I ordered it on DVD for myself. If I am honest, I preferred the days when they came in the post as a surprise because you loved watching my face light up with joy. Now I must make my own joy.

You would have adored it and you would have taken great pleasure watching me adore it. The first episode had an all-star cast and was a clever, extremely meta episode that combined a jewel heist with the commedia dell'arte. Entitled *Wuthering Heist* the jokes were fast and punny. I had at least six snorts and one gasp, so you know it was good.

There were knowing asides to the audience breaking the fourth wall like when the character of Columbina tells us the reason for combining Italian Renaissance theatre with a crime caper is because they both use masks.

Oh, Best Beloved. I laughed harder than I have in ages. Harder than I have since you shuffled off this mortal coil. I wish you were here watching it with me. I can see how we would turn this into our own private language and endlessly quote it to crack each other up. But I am here, and I am laughing for both of us.

All my love,
Heather

Dear Best Beloved,

Today marks seven years since we moved to Wales. What an adventure that was! We had spent a spectacular decade in England but we had the opportunity to move to Wales for even more shenanigans and so we did. That is what I loved about you. You made everything seem like a marvellous adventure.

I remember what it was like packing to move. How had we acquired so much stuff in ten years of living in the United Kingdom? There were nearly 8,000 books and countless pieces of artwork. I love that no matter where we live it feels like I am living in both a library and a museum.

I remember the way that we packed. After every box we successfully filled we rewarded ourselves with an episode of *Doctor Who* which in hindsight was a terrible plan. The night before the removal van was due to arrive, we had a whole host of odd-shaped things that hadn't fit into boxes that we had piled in the back bedroom to think about later. Well, there was no later.

I remember the way we stayed up all night getting more and more hysterical through lack of sleep and laughing so hard that tears squeezed out my eyes watching your antics as you mimed trying to fit yourself into our largest box. I remember how we sealed up the last box full of our possessions just as the sun was rising. Then we remembered the spiders.

We had to get all our darling tarantulas into travel containers as quickly as possible and none of them would behave and cooperate. It was a race against the clock to get all eight of them into travel boxes as I ran the evacuated tanks downstairs to dump the substrate behind a tree and then run back into the house to collect the next tank. We finally got them all into their little boxes and you packed them into our largest flat bottomed shopping bag and ran to catch the train to Wales as I waited for the removal van to arrive. I remember the way your lips lingered on mine, the way we did our secret handshake and you said that you would count the hours until we could be together again.

I think about that train journey. I picture you clutching the bag full of tarantulas close to your body to keep the Spiderbabes safe and to keep other passengers from knowing that you had a bag full of tarantulas. I worried that somehow someone could tell that you were carrying such precious cargo and would be frightened by it. We never wanted to scare anyone, but we also knew that not everyone could see their beauty like we did.

I love that our life was filled with spiders. When I met you in 1989 and found out that you had a tarantula named Shirley MacLaine, I knew right then at that very moment that I wanted to marry you because I adored spiders. My prize possession was a dead tarantula in a jar of formaldehyde that was a gift from a scientist for my tenth birthday. Remember how we used to say that we were too weird for anyone else? I love that we were weird together.

It is interesting that after you died so many people asked if I would leave Wales and move back to the United States. Why would I leave this green and pleasant land where I am surrounded by friends who have become family to me? We dreamed about this life ever since we fell in love, and I would not give up our dream because it keeps me close to you.

All my love,
Heather

22/08/2021

Dear Best Beloved,

I used to love going on holidays with you. In many ways the last nearly eighteen years of living in the United Kingdom has been one long holiday. Here we are, living adventurously, but now it is just me having adventures.

I loved planning a holiday with you. We were like children at a sleepover—staying up late and giggling until our sides were creased with laughter as we planned all the wonderful things we would do and eat and experience. It often centred around a play in the West End of London, or an interesting museum exhibition and we would build outwards planning layer upon layer of activities until we had a full itinerary but with a little wiggle room for surprises. There were always surprises with you. You loved to surprise me. I miss being surprised.

Then I would leave you alone because although the planning was ours to share together, the actual preparations were your domain. When we lived in England, you ordered train tickets online well in advance to ensure a discount and had them posted to the house. Since moving to Wales, we favoured the Megabus that left at 2 a.m. but only cost a tenner to get to London. "More money for adventures," you used to say. The tickets would sit in the middle dresser drawer, and we would open the drawer and peek inside and smile as we counted down the days. You booked the hotel, the

Celtic Hotel with Mrs Marazzi who had been our maternal figure since we were exchange students in 1990. You packed the suitcase. We called it Travel Tetris as you could get a surprising amount of stuff in the smallest of cases. You did this so that we could include things I needed to deal with my chronic pain on the trip like my ergonomic neck pillow. You willingly carried the heavy suitcase to save my back along with your rucksack and often mine as well if I was in pain after travelling so long. You carried it all and never complained. You had such a good sense of direction and always led us where we needed to go. I can get lost going from work to home (true story) and you navigated us with confidence so that I did not have to. You did everything to make my life more comfortable. Who is there for me now?

I had a terrible feeling that if I do not learn how to make my way in the world alone that I will never find the joy that I once had—that I will miss out on life and I know you would want me to thrive not just survive. It is not easy to bloom without you as you were my sun, but I am trying my best.

I decided as it was summer that I should attempt a trip. Suddenly I had to do all the things that you did and let me tell you how hard it was, Best Beloved. I cried the whole time trying to organise a trip to see my Odd-Bod Gang in Gloucestershire.

I have learned how to buy train tickets online. I did not do a particularly good job of it because I somehow accidentally bought not one, not two, but THREE tickets to my destination. So, now I also know how to return train tickets after fighting with Train Line for several weeks. There have been so many tears in the last few weeks—at my foolishness, at how websites like this always confound me, being furious with you for leaving me alone to fend for myself. But I have learned from my mistakes, and it will be better next time.

I had to figure out how to pack in bags that were not too heavy. This was so hard, and I wept to not have my strong man there to look after me. Now no one looks after me but me. But I figured it out.

Thankfully the anxiety of having to navigate on the other end was taken away from me as they met me at the station. I am not ready for navigation.

The trip could not have been better. As soon as I got to their house, I visibly uncoiled from the tense spring that I had been and the crushing pain that has been in my chest since you died eased. We bimbled about town visiting the cute and quirky shops, watched films, listened to Bardcore, ate glorious food from their allotment and made bunting for their garden out of charity shop shirts. It was just what I needed.

I cried on the train on the way home and snotted in my mask when they unexpectedly made me change trains in Cardiff. But I managed it.

I did it. I figured it out. I managed to do it on my own, even though I know you were tucked away in my heart. It let me know that my life does not have to end here without you. That with each skill I learn, with each fear I overcome that I will be able to live adventurously again. I would give anything to do it with you, but that is not the choice I have been given. I am trying hard to move from just surviving and counting the days until we meet again to thriving. It is the hardest thing I have ever done. But I will get there, Best Beloved. You watch me go.

All my love,
Heather

Dear Best Beloved,

We had book club tonight. We were reading Matt Haig's *The Midnight Library* where the protagonist gets to see all the variations of her life that might have happened if she had made different choices. This was a hard book for me to get through.

I kept thinking that somewhere out there you are still alive, that we made some other choice—perhaps you articulated to me more clearly just how poorly you were feeling, and I made you go to see our GP sooner. But then I also thought that there must be a life out there where you died the first time you had cancer. That was certainly a possibility. I could have lost you then after only four years of marriage, but instead we were granted twenty-four more years. Imagine if you had died in 1996-1997—all the things we would have never done. I would still be living in Louisiana as I am certain I would never have been brave enough to emigrate without you. We were able to have so many adventures because of the additional time we were granted.

Do I wish that we had more time? Of course. I expected that we would grow old together. But we crammed so many amazing adventures into these last twenty-five years and for that I am thankful. There are so many people out there who will never have, even for a moment, what we had. There are people who dream about changing their lives, but are too afraid to take that first step. You made me brave. You made me feel like we could change the world.

And we did.

All my love,
Heather

SEPTEMBER

03/09/2021

Dear Best Beloved,

You left me a list of things I needed to remember to do after you died. You wrote it in that microscopic scrawl of yours that was only beginning to show signs that you were ravaged with cancer. A few days later when we were trying to make a will, I was afraid you would not be able to write your name as it was clear you were descending at a break-neck speed towards your death. You did manage it, but you paused after every letter and looked up at me with the most pitiful expression to ask me what letter came next. It broke both our hearts that you could not remember how to spell your own name.

This note was the perfect combination of our two personalities—you being fastidiously organised and me being haphazard and careless. You wrote it on the merest scrap of paper (the back of an old envelope) that was destined to get lost or be mistaken for rubbish and recycled by me. Luckily, I did not lose it or dispose of it as I have been known to do. I pinned it to the cork board as I knew that it was important.

The top of the list was to remind me to renew my British passport because it expired at the end of September. You told me to start dealing with it at the beginning of this month and so I am doing it. Every time we have ever had to do anything like this it was you who searched for the forms, printed them out at work, filled them in, and posted them to the correct address. All I had to do was sign my name on the form you had prepared earlier. I willingly let you do this because I hate filling out forms, especially forms where you have to put one capital letter in each box. Those sorts of forms send my anxiety into overdrive. But since you departed this world and left me alone, I have learned to do it. I still do not like it, but I am capable of doing it.

I decided to do the online form as it was £10 cheaper, and I could not figure out how to get a paper copy. I know you would have frowned at that as you didn't trust doing things online and preferred to have good old-fashioned pen and paper, but I have to make things work my own way. It said that I must send my current British passport as well as any other passport that I held from another country and so I had to send my American passport as well. I could feel myself unspooling as I played the frightful "What If" game. What if I have done this all wrong? What if they lose my American Passport? What if the photos I had taken yesterday at the key cutting place are rejected?

I paid online and they took my money, so I suppose that means I did it correctly. Time will tell.

All my love,
Heather

Dear Best Beloved,

I had to go to the shop to film the storytelling for the shop's YouTube channel today. These are days that I dread, because you are not here with me, Best Beloved. It is not the mechanics of it—after nearly six months I know how to film it on my own. I have mastered the art of how to prop up my phone on the bookshelf instead of the complicated way you used to do it involving a table and a stack of books. I know how to edit out the bits of me walking to and from the camera after it has been laid in the exact right position. What I miss is YOU. This was always something we did together, even if I was could do it on my own. You would come because I liked the support. I only had to say, "Would you please come help me film on Sunday?" and you would smile (a radiant smile you saved for my eyes only) and kiss my forehead and reply, "But of course, Madame. What is an actress without her trusty cameraman?"

I always suspected I could probably do it all by myself, but it gave you as much pleasure as it did me—another example of how we complimented each other. It is these times where we went together, and you set up the camera as I waited on my mark ready to begin as soon as you gave the word that I treasure because they are the only recordings I have of your voice. I can hear you say, "At your leisure," and "It looks like it is recording," and "When you're ready." These are all the words I have from you. I miss that soft drawl and the love that is evident in these small phrases because what they really mean is "I love you and I am proud to support you."

So, it is days like today that I find difficult. But the show must go on, as they say. At noon I went to the shop in the drizzle and set everything up as it should be and recorded the story of *Mr Wiggle and Mr Waggle*. Afterwards, I sat down in the comfortable wingback chair to review the footage and see if I needed to record it a second time. There was a curious beam of light that came from the ceiling and shone directly in my face. It was clear on the video, but when I looked at the space with my eyes, I could detect no strange illumination other than the florescent lights. Where did it come from? I repositioned both myself and the camera and performed the story again. When I went to review the footage, it was there again—a beam of light that shone right in my face that only appeared in the film.

All I can think of is that it is you. I want it to be you, Best Beloved. Please let it be you telling me that you are still here lighting my way.

All my love,
Heather

14/09/2021

Dear Best Beloved,

I am trying to take a leaf out of your book and be organised and plan ahead. I contacted Co-op Funeralcare and asked to prepay for my own cremation so when my time comes it will be taken care of. This was harder than I expected it to be. Having to contact them again, having to reiterate that I understood that you didn't get a funeral with direct cremation because I had recently done it for you. I had to agree that it was my responsibility before I died to arrange for someone to collect my ashes and bring them to the place where you are buried, and here is where I became overwrought. When you died, I was there for you. I was there for you every moment of your last few days and I held your hand as you passed from this life to the next. But who will be there for me? Who will be there to hold my hand when I die so I won't be afraid? I came to the awful realisation that I will die alone with no one who loves me by my side. This is the wretched truth about being the survivor. You had me, but I have nobody.

All my love,
Heather

23/09/2021

Dear Best Beloved,

My heart still feels like an open wound. It feels raw and sore continually pecked open by the carrion crows of grief. I can feel it start to scab over—that in itself is a painful drawing process as the edges of my life knit together without you—then suddenly I am caught off guard and the scab is unceremoniously ripped from my beating heart and my grief is open and wide again.

I find myself obsessing over "What If" which I know is not helpful, but I cannot seem to stop. The deeper I get into this pit of despair the more I think I failed you.

I knew something was wrong, I just couldn't put my finger on it. You felt distant. Not yourself. But I wasn't myself either. Lockdown had a terrible effect on our mental health. I remember saying to you, "I can't find you. You feel far away," and you held my hand and replied, "I'm right here."

But you weren't. You were somewhere else. You wanted to sleep all the time and we stopped having sex. You spent every day in your dressing gown and didn't bother to get dressed. I thought you were depressed, but you denied it. You insisted that it was me who was depressed, and you were right. But something undefinable was definitely wrong with you. Did you know then? Did you have an inkling that there was something rotten in the state of Denmark?

When did you know, and did you bury your head in the sand because you didn't want to think about the possibility that your cancer had returned? How long had you felt unwell before you told me in January about the pain in your side?

Thomas Roy Pitchford, why didn't you bloody say something sooner? And then when you did tell me about the mysterious stitch in your side, I didn't believe you. I thought it was because you were working from home and spending all day sitting in that weird hunched over position on the sofa typing on your laptop. I kept telling you that if you were getting a stitch you should move to the desk or at the very least prop yourself up with a pillow. But you—being you—were so stubborn and were determined not to heed any of my good advice. You just sat on the sofa being in pain. Were you trying to tell me in some roundabout way that you knew something was wrong?

Were you afraid? I think you must have been. Do you remember how hard I had to work on you to get you to call our GP? I kept saying in the most dismissive tone, "It can't be hurting that bad if you won't call the doctor!" Was I afraid? I think I was so deep in denial about the fact that this could be serious that I just opted to be angry. I was angry a lot in 2020 and I am so sorry.

I just keep picking at the scab thinking if we both hadn't been so stubborn would we have sought treatment earlier and saved your life?

All my love,
Heather

25/09/2021

Dear Best Beloved,

I wish that 2020 had not been our last year together. Neither of us were at our best. We had such a happy life together, but that year—that awful year—we were at our worst. At least I was. This is a scab I keep picking until it bleeds. I keep obsessively thinking about that year and how I was feeling and how unfair I was to you.

I was angry at the situation because I found the isolation difficult. I was on furlough with nothing to do and you were working from home. The lockdown happened so quickly that I didn't have time to stock up on any craft materials or fabric to have a project to work on. We both know I need routine and something to do or I am LOST. I had neither and I was rudderless and the fact that you still had a job you could do from home (even if you weren't particularly happy doing it) made me feel like Vesuvius on the verge of erupting every minute of the day.

I remember seething on the stairs, my jaw clenched tightly and if I had been a cartoon character steam would have been coming out of my ears. Everything I did irritated you. I was stomping around the house like an elephant or sighing and humphing in a way that put you off your work. You kept telling me to leave the room because I was distracting you and so I would go and sit on the stairs and think hateful thoughts about you.

I am so ashamed of that. It was only because the one thing I could think of to work on was my writing and I needed the laptop for that. But I couldn't have the laptop, could I? No, because you needed it for work. And so, I would stomp from room to room huffing and puffing, waiting until you were finished work so that it could be MY TURN. Then after work you wanted to unwind by playing games on the laptop. I was consumed with thoughts that you were SELFISH. That you could not share. I am sure you will never forget the meltdown that I had where I must have looked like a toddler who needed a nap. You were taken very much by surprise at the depth of my feelings. In January we bought a second laptop, and it was like a weight was lifted off my shoulders. No more sulking and skulking about the house. Despite complaining of pain when you typed while sitting on the sofa you refused to sit at the desk and so I set myself up there and worked happily on writing short stories while you attended countless Zoom meetings.

I wish that I could apologise to you in person and make it up to you. I worry that you died thinking I didn't love you or that I only loved you because you bought me my own laptop.

All my love,
Heather

28/09/2021

Dear Best Beloved,

Last night I noticed a pain in my side. My right side. Just like you had. It hurt when I took a deep breath, and I got a shooting pain when I raised my arm above my head. I lay in bed scanning my whole body for any niggle, any sense that something was wrong. I tried to remember what you said, how you felt. You said it hurt when you bent over and hurt when you stretched up. My heart thrummed in my chest so strongly I could feel the pulse at my temple beating. It seemed to spell out CAN-CER, CAN-CER, CAN-CER. Had my grief caused my cells to mutate and poison my body? Would a scan reveal that like you, cancer had metastasised to my liver?

I started to imagine what I would do. Would chemotherapy save me or like you, would it be too late? What if it could possibly save my life, would I take it? Or would I say, "No thank you. My husband died in March, and I would like to pass up lifesaving treatment to join him."

I began to visualise the faces of people who loved me and the disappointment they would feel if I chose to throw my life away. I decided that I would do nothing. I would pretend to be you and ignore it like an ostrich, burying my head in the sand so if it was cancer no one could blame me if it turned out to be too late.

I went to bed and dreamed that I was dying (beautifully and

bravely like Beth in *Little Women*) and that you were waiting for me on the Other Side.

But then I awoke and as always, I am still here. The pain in my side is much better. In hindsight, I have probably just pulled a muscle because I lifted several crates of heavy books recently at work and yesterday, I was shelving books over my head standing on my tiptoes because I was too lazy to get the stepladder.

Oh Thomas, how do I manage to do this sort of thing and get derailed by a runaway train of thought? You used to sigh and say, "Oh Alice, you've done it again." Alice was our code word for going down a rabbit hole of unhelpful thoughts. Yes, I was being Alice and had gone quite mad for a moment. If you were here, you would have spotted the signs sooner before I was swept away.

But here's the thing—this morning when I woke up my first thought was not disappointment. I wasn't crushed to still be alive because I was thinking about all the people who love me and realised that I love them back. I reflected that I would miss them and though I cannot wait until our sweet reunion, a part of me wants to stay here. To stay alive.

So, I guess that is progress.

All my love,
Heather

30/09/2021

Dear Best Beloved,

Well, I must have done it right because when I got home from work my new passport was waiting for me. I know that I over-reacted when it was time to renew it, but it just felt like all the things I hate—filling in forms, paying online, and waiting.

As I have waited this very long month, I had time to reflect on it and realised that I will need to be much more self-aware now that you are gone. You often recognised unhelpful behaviours in me before I realised that I was doing it. You had a wonderful way of approaching my mental health lightly, turning the problem on its head and making a joke. You imitated my behaviour in a hysterical over the top style that helped me understand just how ridiculous I was behaving.

I think of you acting like the tutu wearing hippo from Disney's *Fantasia* leaping about the room pretending to be me jumping to conclusions. All you had to do was get your feet into ballet first position with your arms in graceful arcs to let me know that I might be overreacting. It never failed to make me dissolve into giggles and helped me to be better.

I have completed one task from your list, and I feel quite proud of myself. You being you, also included on the list that I will need to renew my American passport in 2028. That one will be far scarier as it not only involves filling out forms but also making an appointment at the American Embassy and then getting to London. Luckily, I have seven years to get braver.

All my love,
Heather

OCTOBER

Dear Best Beloved,

I still dread any correspondence addressed to you. My friends have said I should just see it as a "wink" from the afterlife, but I just cannot seem to do it. It doesn't feel like a nice little message from you, but rather an ice-pick to the heart.

There were two today. There was a letter addressed to you from British Telecom. It said that they had tried to email you repeatedly and you were not responding. This one made me furious because I have called BT on no less than four other occasions to remind them that you are dead, get the account put into my name and change the email contact because I am locked out of the email you attached to the account. Every time I do this a seemingly helpful person assures me that all my details have been updated and then every few months you get another letter.

In the past I have let my anger overwhelm me and I have shouted at a salesperson when it wasn't their fault. Do you remember the meltdown I had in the tile store in 1995 when they had the perfect tiles that I wanted for our bathroom, and it turned out that style was discontinued but they still had a sample on display? I feel such deep shame and regret over my behaviour that day, even all these years later. I NEVER want to be that kind of person again. But how was I going to get through to BT? In the end I cried. I sobbed on the phone and let grief overtake me instead of anger. This time I think it will stick. She credited my account £25 for the stress that it caused me.

Then I had an email from Page 45 Comics. I had already had the experience of having Issue Two of the *Locke and Key/Sandman* crossover appear on our doorstep. It was shocking at first, but that was more like a wink from you beyond the grave. I should have known you pre-ordered it. You wanted to make sure we would get it as soon as possible. I was afraid to open the email. I just stared at the subject line which read: *trouble with your account*. When I did finally open the email, it said that you had pre-ordered a comic and when they tried to take money from the debit card that they had on file it was declined. And so, twice in one morning, I had to phone up and explain that you were dead.

They were very sympathetic and agreed to cancel the order. I had no idea that you had pre-ordered the third instalment of the *Locke and Key/Sandman* crossover. I didn't know that you could pre-order something that far in advance. I suppose I should have realised that you would have been so organised as the keeper of dates, but in my new role as the one who does the ordering, I pre-ordered it last month from Forbidden Planet.

And so, I have worked hard to get rid of you with BT and strike you from their files and then I found you again with Page 45 as I carry on our love for comics.

All my love,
Heather

Dear Best Beloved,

It was your American memorial service today. They held it where your mother grew up in Campti at Coulee Bethel Baptist Church. Thank goodness for technology so that I could watch it via video call on my phone. I just didn't feel the time was right to fly all the way back to Louisiana, especially with Covid rates still surging. I know how you felt about that. You were adamant that when you died, we mustn't have any kind of gathering for you because it could put people's lives in danger. Thankfully, I could stay home and watch in it on my phone through the wonders of modern video technology while others sat far apart and wore masks.

I wondered if I would feel sad, if I would be overwhelmed with grief listening to your family reminisce about your life. And I did, but not for the reason I was expecting.

It was painfully clear that they did not know you at all. They talked extensively about your love for Pooh Bear that you had at the age of four, but no one could come up with any stories about your adult life. I pity them that they never found out just what a remarkable man you were.

They never knew how hilarious you were. Your favourite trick was to whisper something in my ear to make me laugh (and occasionally snort) as you pretended to be innocent and had no idea why that mad woman beside you was howling with laughter. Your myriad of impressions always kept me entertained. It began with Francis the Talking Napkin Holder and the Syllabus (the Silly Bus as he was known) when we were in college and extended to such greats as acting out Crimes Against Hugh Manatee. The fact that you did a convincing manatee impression still makes me chortle.

They never knew how incredibly lucky you were. You just had a knack for competitions. I will never forget when we still lived in Louisiana you won us an all-expense paid trip to Arizona for a murder mystery weekend from A&E Mysteries. It was a hoot and we ended up being suspects due to my acting abilities and because so many people thought we were the murderers we won a trophy. Or the time you won us tickets from a radio call-in competition to see The Moody Blues in concert backed by the Baton Rouge Symphony. Then the pièce de résistance when you won us two plane tickets to London on British Airways by completing a quiz on Cockney rhyming slang. It was on that trip that a man vomited on me, and we got bumped up to first class because I didn't make a fuss. I managed to dodge most of it and having been a first-grade teacher was no stranger to bodily fluids. Just like everything in our lives it became part of our story and something to laugh about.

You just had a way of charming people into giving us fun experiences like when you wrote to producer John Lloyd and said we had tickets to a recording of the BBC television programme *QI* on our wedding anniversary and could we do something special. John Lloyd replied and graciously offered us backstage passes to meet the cast and that is how we met Stephen Fry who was incredibly humble. He introduced himself as, "Hello my name is Stephen. It is nice to meet you." I still can't believe we got to do that.

I was so touched when you were dying and Chris Ryall from IDW Comics got together with Joe Hill the author of our beloved *Locke and Key* and Skelton Crew the lovely people who make the replica keys and sent us a care package. It wasn't the first time Chris had sent us cool *Locke and Key* merch, but I was very humbled by their concern for us at the end.

They never knew what an amazing gift-giver you were. You would spend all year planning some fantastic surprise for me because you knew how happy it made me. Your gifts were clever and personal. Probably my favourite gift I ever received from you was the year that you wrote to all my favourite children's authors and illustrators and asked them to send me a birthday card. On my twenty-eighth birthday you presented me with an album full of personalised notes from the likes of Trina Schart Hyman who drew me the most delightful illustration of Ladybug and Pussywillow from *Cricket Magazine*, Eric Carle who drew me *The Very Hungry Caterpillar* as well as Norman Bridwell who drew me a picture of *Clifford the Big Red Dog*. There were almost a hundred letters in there and that became the start of our autograph collection.

They never knew how smart you were, what an excellent researcher you were. You had such a breadth of knowledge about so many subjects. You were fascinating to listen to if someone could get you talking which was rare. You preferred to be a listener most of the time which is probably why we got along so well.

They never knew about your "fifteen minutes of fame" when you discovered that a poem being taught in schools all over the world had been misattributed to the great 19th century poet William Blake. The dedication and dogged researching that you did to trace the mistake back to its original source in the *Times Educational Supplement* still amazes me. You even got interviewed on BBC News! You also got a mention in a book by Dave Gorman all about the "Fake Blake" and the dangers of not checking your sources. You would never have brought this up in conversation as you were as modest as you were brilliant, but I knew. I knew what a genius you were.

I feel very sorry for them that they never knew you, but I am so glad that I did. I am eternally thankful that I had you in my life for thirty-two wonderful years.

All my love,
Heather

17/10/2021

Dear Best Beloved,

One of the things I loved about you was that you were just as passionate about art and children's literature as I was. Our trips to London always included a museum exhibition or two.

The last time we went to London was a year before the pandemic. I desperately want to go back, but I still feel this is not the right time to go. Covid is still surging and once I was there, I would have to navigate my way around the big city, and I can get lost on an escalator (as you used to say). It is harder without you and your memory for directions. Do you remember when we went back to London ten years after we were exchange students to ring in the new year 2000—all that worry about Y2K for nothing! You said to me, "Do you know where we are?" No, of course I didn't. "We used to walk this way to classes every day ten years ago. Surely you must remember?" You expected me to remember some place I couldn't find in 1990 a decade later. I think this is where you really begin to realise just how poor my sense of direction was.

I saw that our favourite museum the V&A was having an *Alice in Wonderland* exhibition. How we would have loved to see that! Art and one of our favourite children's books combined! If you were alive, we would have planned a holiday around the exhibition. It was another thing that weighed heavily on me. Will I ever get to do those things again? Is that part of my life over?

I was so keen to see it, but I am not ready to face the big city without you. Then suddenly, I saw an advert on Facebook. I know you were always slightly paranoid about our computers listening in on our secret conversations and then showing us related advertising. But honestly, I hadn't said anything out loud, I just wished it in my heart. Because of the pandemic, many other people would also like to attend this exhibition but like me they could not. The V&A filmed a tour of the exhibit which included interviews with artists and illustrators who have taken their turn to create their own version of Lewis Carroll's famous book. I held my breath. Would our local cinema be showing it? It was! There was one showing today at 2:30 p.m. and so I promptly bought myself a ticket online.

I stopped off at the shop Flying Tiger before the show to buy a raspberry lemonade and impulsively bought a crown of spiders (as you do) from the Halloween display and wore it on my head as I sat in the dark and pretended that we were in London seeing it together. Was it as good as going to the big city with you? No. Nothing ever is. But it was a good experience and made me feel like that part of my life is not over. It may not be how I thought it would be, but like everything these days I just have to adapt.

Perhaps someday I will go to London again. Perhaps I will find a friend who likes museums who would like to go with me. London is much more fun with two. I shall look for a suitable travel companion and see if I can find a way to continue the things that brought us joy together. But if I am never brave enough to go, there's always the cinema. At least going there, I can't get lost!

All my love,
Heather

Dear Best Beloved,

I have noticed lately that I don't seem to be holding tension in my body the way I did right after you died. My chronic pain is better and the feeling of a clamp on my larynx that crushed my throat anytime I had to speak about you has gone. When did it go? How have I not noticed?

Suddenly today I just dropped you into conversation as easy as pie (or as easy as cake as you always said) and nothing happened. My body did not revolt against me. My throat did not squeeze me like an accordion making my voice bray out like a bereaved donkey. I even laughed as I told the story about the one and only time that I had an espresso and then was so hyped up I race-walked to Hitchin Boys School and walked around and around your library desk while you began to tally just how many times that I galloped around you all the while talking a mile-a-minute and gesticulating wildly. Finally, after going around for the two- hundredth time you stopped me and asked if I was on drugs. Every time after that whenever I showed any interest in caffeinated coffee you would do an impression of me that was ridiculously over the top and then I would squeal and pretend to be you and say in your best deadpan voice, "Heather Elizabeth Tisdale, are you on DRUGS?" and then we would both fall about laughing.

It was such a happy memory and it felt good to feel it. I want to remember you that way, silly and protective of me at the same time. I don't want to think of you as jaundiced and furious like you were in your last days. By the end you were so yellow that you looked like you should have been on *The Simpsons*. If it weren't so tragic, it would have been hilarious.

I hope there will be more days like this.

All my love,
Heather

24/10/2021

Dear Best Beloved,

I went to the shops today, Tesco followed by Lidl. Both times I used a trolley with wheels instead of a basket because why wouldn't I? It makes shopping so much easier. But you wouldn't. What was this grudge you had against wheeled supermarket trollies? When did it start? I wish I could remember. I don't recall you being like this when we lived in England. When did it begin in Wales?

It was only when I realised that shopping is so much easier without you that I began to really reflect on how irritating this obsession was. You insisted that we weren't doing a big shop and so it only needed to be a small basket that you could carry by hand rather than a larger wheeled trolley. I remember you glaring at me if I suggested buying a second carton of soya milk as you strained under the weight of it with that ridiculously small basket. When Lidl switched from the metal basket that dug into your arm as you carried it to the small kind that wheeled behind you a bit like a suitcase you insisted on lifting that basket and carrying it awkwardly in the crook of your arm rather than sensibly wheeling it behind you. Why were you like this, my difficult darling?

Because you insisted on using the small wire basket, I had to make four separate shopping lists each week: two for Tesco (now and later) and two for Lidl (now and later.) It would take me hours to make the lists each week. Even with the annoying habit of the multiple lists and your ridiculous trolley allergy, it was still something we looked forward to doing together. You could make the most mundane of tasks exciting and we had many supermarket games like "look at that disgusting thing" where we tried to draw the other person's eye toward something like squid in a jar and "surely that's vegan" when pointing to something that most definitely was not.

Then the pandemic hit, and everything changed. Supermarkets insisted that a person must shop alone, and you were the strong one in our family, so it had to be you. It was the only time you ever left the house in 2020. I remember having a meltdown when you came home with one bunch of spring onions as a substitute for a kilogram of red onions. "How can one bunch of spring onions feed us for a week?" I screamed at you. You seemed incapable of making any decisions which I now wonder if that was the creeping in of your illness and we just didn't realise it. I thought you were purposely being obtuse just to vex me. I am so very sorry for the way I behaved. I wish you were here so that I could apologise again.

Now not only did I have to write four lists, but every item had to have a first, second and third choice as there were food shortages and I wasn't there to suggest a suitable alternative. It was exhausting.

All of this has made me realise that I am glad that I remember you properly and not just through rose-tinted spectacles. I remember the good (and there was so much good) and the bad and the ugly. You were wonderful as well as exasperating and I wouldn't trade a minute of it.

All my love,
Heather

26/10/2021

Dear Best Beloved,

I haven't cried in days. It shocked me when I realised it. In the beginning I was proud if I could get through the day without crying in public, but now I hardly cry at all. I still do if something takes me by surprise like an unexpected letter or a task I don't know how to do. But let's be honest, those things might have made me cry when you were alive.

In the beginning grief was so heavy, like a huge boulder that I had to endlessly roll up a hill like Sisyphus. Every day the task would be too great, and the boulder and I would come crashing down, limp and weakened by the weight of life. But these days are different. I have learned to carve that boulder into manageable chunks, so I don't carry it all at one time. But I still carry it. My grief boulder never leaves me but these days I carry it in my trolley instead of on my shoulders. I roll it behind me, feel its weight, and keep moving forward.

All my love,
Heather

NOVEMBER

02/11/2021

Dear Best Beloved,

I was listening to the soundtrack of the musical *Hamilton* and in the song *Who Lives, Who Dies, Who Tells Your Story* Alexander Hamilton's widow sings:

"I stop wasting time on tears. I live another fifty years."

I hear these words for the first time, and I suddenly feel so despondent. Every night before bed I say it is one more day until I am reunited with you. I am counting the days until I can see you again, my Best Beloved.

I am not sure I can be as brave as Eliza Hamilton and wait that long.

But I must. And so, I will carry on as she did. I will do good in the world and always tell your story. Our story. My story.

All my love,
Heather

09/11/2021

Dear Best Beloved,

You know I have always wanted a pet I can cuddle but having severe allergies to fur, dander and saliva has put quite a damper on those dreams. It is hard to be an animal lover who can't be around animals.

I think this is why I transferred my affection to spiders. You can't hug them (you shouldn't even handle them according to the British Tarantula Society) but you can love them and study their behaviour. This is just one of the many reasons I fell in love with you. You loved our Spiderbabes, too.

On this day in 2017, you went for an interview to be a weekend Butterfly Ranger (Or Butt Wrangler as you jokingly called it) at the National Botanic Garden of Wales. You came home from the interview, opened the door, and called out my name. I bounded out of the room to greet you and noticed you were carrying a suspicious parcel. You were grinning madly at me and told me to go sit in the living room and close my eyes. Oh, the suspense of it! I was used to you bringing home all kinds of interesting things so I couldn't wait for the surprise. You pulled out a small plastic container with airholes. Whatever I was expecting to be in the box, it was not this. You opened the lid and there inside were the three cutest snails I had ever seen. It was love at first sight! Finally, a pet I could hold!

You told me that they were Giant African Land Snails and would grow to be quite big. Giant snails! Could it get any better? It was only then that I thought to ask if you had gotten the job. I wondered if they had rejected you but sent you away with a gastropod consolation prize. But no, you got both the job and the snails.

But what to name them? All our pets had literary or artistic names. There were three of them. I immediately thought of *The Mikado* and began to sing, "Three little snails from school are we." But then we thought naming a snail Yum-Yum was quite cruel since escargot are eaten, so that was rejected. Suddenly your face lit up and you got a twinkle in your eye, and I knew whatever you said would be perfect. And it was. Anne, Charlotte, and Emily—The Brontë Snails.

You were right, they are massive now. Each one weighs about 300 grams and their shell is as big as my hand. I love to hold them and give them a bath. I love the way they rasp my skin with their mouth like being licked by a cat with its sandpapery tongue. I love that you brought them home to me four years ago so that I could have a pet to cuddle. I loved the way you talked to our pets and then made them answer in funny voices—high and squeaky for the Spiderbabes and low and slooooow for the Brontë Snails. I love them because like the Spiderbabes, they connect me to you and your immense love for all creatures great and small. It feels so good to remember our unconventional life together.

All my love,
Heather

12/11/2021

Dear Best Beloved,

You often made things very complicated. After you died, I set the alarm clock to the actual time. Not some unspecified amount of time ahead of the actual time. How far ahead? I didn't know. I don't think you did either. Why did you do this? I have no idea. I can remember when we needed to set the clock for an earlier time than our normal time. I would watch you with your furrowed brow mentally counting how far ahead you thought it might be and then subtracting some time and adding other time and hemming and hawing about whether the clock was set for the right time. Inevitably, we would either wake up slightly early or ridiculously early (like before sunrise) because you had no idea how far ahead the clock was from the real time. Why were you like this, Best Beloved? Why did you make everything so hard? After you died, I set every clock in the house to the correct time. I could almost hear your disapproving humph. At least now I know what time it is since all the clocks are set the same.

I love you so much, but sometimes you were very hard to live with.

All my love,
Heather

21/11/2021

Dear Best Beloved,

Such adventures I have had! A few weeks ago, I got an email from our friend Karen in Newcastle asking me if I would like to join her for a very quick one-night stay in Bath (or "Bahth" as you liked to call it when you used your posh voice) as an early birthday treat. She sent my train ticket to me through the post which helped me to avoid the issues I had in August when I accidentally bought three tickets due to my inexperience buying tickets online.

There was a small *Pre-Raphaelite* exhibit at the Holburne Museum all about the portraits of the artist Dante Gabriel Rossetti. There was also a fashion museum. How could I resist?

I remember when we first discovered the *Pre-Raphaelite Movement*. It was the 20th of February 1990. It was our one-year anniversary and we had gone to lunch at the Café in the Crypt at St-Martin-in-the-Fields. After eating we ambled to the giftshop, and I found a postcard of a stunning sorrowful red-haired maiden in a boat. I remember saying to you, "Doesn't this look like that poem by Tennyson?" and lo and behold, it was. It was John Waterhouse's 1888 painting of *The Lady of Shalott*. The following Monday (hot on the heels of our recent engagement) we went to the Tate Gallery and asked our art teacher to please take us to the painting so that I could see it in person. She told us that the painter Waterhouse was at the tail end of an art movement with a group of artists who called themselves the *Pre-Raphaelite Brotherhood* and if I loved lush paintings based on literature, we should check them out. And check them out we did. Over the years we have visited every museum in the United Kingdom that housed some of their paintings. You also found me autographs of the three founding members of the Brotherhood—Dante Gabriel Rossetti, William Holman Hunt and John Millais as well as five of their followers. We have a whole bookcase of books about their art. When I think of them, I think of you.

We both arrived in Bath yesterday around noon and made our way straight to the museum. Oh, it was glorious to see Rossetti's paintings and sketches of Lizzie Siddal, Fanny Cornforth, and Jane Morris. There were several I had never seen before. Then we went to find the YMCA youth hostel (it's fun to stay at the YMCA) and out for a bite to eat. We ate at a quirky vegan restaurant, wandered around Mr B's Emporium of Reading Delights, and then just strolled out in the frosty air looking at the Christmas lights which had been put up far too soon as it is not even December. This morning we got up early and went to the Fashion Museum to see all the beautiful clothes and an interesting shoe exhibit then to Persephone the feminist bookshop and finally it was back to the station and on our way home.

On the way home everything that could possibly go wrong went wrong. My train was cancelled, then when the next train appeared an hour later there were only two coaches and it was already heaving with people. I managed to squeeze on but could not get a seat, so just faced the wall like a naughty child to try not to get breathed on by all the unmasked folks around me. When I got to my connection in Cardiff there was a platform change and then halfway home, they told me I had to get to the other end of the train because it was going to divide. All my fears had come at once and I tried to think WWTD—What Would Thomas Do? When I was the old me, I thought you were quite cool and confident about such things. You always looked so serious and decisive as you navigated unexpected changes. But now that I am doing it by myself, I think you were more scared than you let on. I know you hated change and your outer demeaner was masking how exhausting it is to navigate those changes in travel plans. I think you worked hard to stay calm for me. You didn't want me to feel anxious and so you pretended to be more confident than you really felt. So, that is exactly what I did. And do you know what? I made it home safely.

Being on this trip made me realise that you were everything to me. You were my museum person, my bookshop person, my theatre person, and my comic convention person. But maybe I don't have to stop doing these things. Maybe I can find different people to fill the different roles in my life. Maybe Karen will be my museum friend. Maybe Kirsty will be my bookshop friend. Maybe Emma will be my theatre friend. Maybe Helen and her lovely family will be my comic convention friends. You will never be able to be replaced, but maybe I can find a way to still experience all the things we loved with friends, and you will still be there because I will carry you in my heart.

All my love,
Heather

24/11/2021

Dear Best Beloved,

You were one of the most positive people I ever knew, but you also had a pessimistic streak. I just chalked it up to some of your weird quirks. There were things that you really took against, and no amount of gentle persuasion could get you to change your mind. You really had it in for online banking and PayPal. Every time I brought them up you would regale me with the tale of someone you had heard about who had something vaguely sinister happen to them when dealing with those services. It was like an urban myth where your stepbrother's neighbour's second cousin once removed knew a guy who knew a woman that had a hook-handed killer in her town.

When you got an idea in your head there was no shifting it. At college when you worked in the library, you became convinced that the metal detector that beeped if you were stealing a book would also erase your cassette tapes and so you made everyone hand over their Walkman and you would return it on the other side of the door. I don't think it was ever proven (in fact, I am pretty sure it was disproven) but you remained convinced until the day you died.

You were strangely both very good with technology and extremely mistrustful of it. You refused to have a smart phone and got by with my crappy old Nokia. You used the outdated tablet that ran so slowly despite me saying that a smart phone was like a mini tablet and would run faster on more current technology. Nope. You wouldn't budge.

There were times when I would say that I wanted to do something like start a blog or help a friend build a website and you were quite discouraging about it. You just kept naming all the possible things that could go wrong. It was strange, because normally you were my biggest fan. You believed I could do things that even I sometimes didn't think I was capable of. So why were you so negative about certain things?

I have pondered this over and over since your death. I think it was because you were afraid. Afraid that you would not be able to help me. Our roles that we had developed over the years were that you were the one who was good at tech, and I was the dramatic one. But every time I suggested something outside your comfort zone you became the overly dramatic one and thought up every excuse in the book to dissuade me from trying. You always ended with, "Well, you can do it, but don't expect any help from me!" And so, I didn't ask for help and it turned out that I was also good at tech.

My difficult darling, why didn't you just say that you didn't know?

All my love,
Heather

DECEMBER

05/12/2021

Dear Best Beloved,

It's a week until my birthday and the weight of getting a year older when you never will is weighing heavily on my heart. Even dressing up as an elf for work has not made me feel happy. I was thinking of our little rituals that we used to do. Those funny little games we played. The way in the week before my birthday you would whistle the first line of the song *Happy Birthday to You*, and I would boing up and down with glee and grin like the Cheshire Cat. Then you would put on a mock surprised face with that twinkle in your eye and say, "What?? I didn't say anything!" and we would both laugh and do our secret handshake. Because of course we had a secret handshake.

Every year on my birthday we always do the same thing— eat leek and potato soup, put up the Christmas tree, and watch *The Muppets Christmas Carol*. We did those rituals for twenty-nine years (the first year we actually saw the film at the Dollar Cinema before buying it on videotape then later DVD) and I don't know what I want to do. Do I keep with tradition to try to hold you close to me or will it make me feel like you are further away?

All my love,
Heather

10/12/2021

Dear Best Beloved,

In the end I decided to break up my birthday traditions into manageable chunks so it wouldn't feel so overwhelming without you. I decided to put up our "Charlie Brown" Christmas tree a day early. I remember when we had lived in England for a year and suddenly realised that we needed a tree. We took the train to Stevenage (which seemed like such a big city to me!) and bought a small three-foot-tall tree for the princely sum of £2.77 at Tesco. Every year we would say, "Next year we'll get a bigger tree!" but we never did.

We have bought an ornament for every Christmas of our married life so this would have been our thirtieth Christmas as a married couple. I debated about whether I wanted to buy one for this year and decided I would. I chose a beautiful wooden snowflake with "Nadolig Llawen" on it and dedicated it to you. I carefully unwrapped every ornament and every memory and hung them on the tree. I want to be able to look back with joy on our life together and not become bitter because of the years we will not get to share. I love our tiny tree in the corner by the bookshelves next to our *Wizard of Oz* and *Locke and Key* collections.

I will have leek and potato soup on Saturday and Sunday (and possibly Monday) and then I will start a new birthday tradition and take myself to the cinema on Sunday to see *West Side Story* It is hard to grow older when you never will but every birthday that I have brings me one step closer to our reunion. I love you with all my heart, Best Beloved.

All my love,
Heather

11/12/2021

Dear Best Beloved,

It's my birthday today. I am fifty-two years old, just like you are. Normally this would be the two-month window where we were briefly the same age before you moved up a year and left me behind. Next year I will leave you behind.

I feel both settled and unsettled, my love. I am happy with the plans I have made for myself. I decorated the tree last night and have felt nostalgic but not melancholy. I have enjoyed my leek and potato soup (and will again, one of the few perks of living alone is left-overs) and am looking forward to seeing *West Side Story* tomorrow. I wonder if you were alive would you have gone with me? Sometimes you humoured me and went places you had no interest in like going to the Pantomime. You really hated all the noise and terrible jokes, but you knew I loved it and screamed with laughter and shouted myself hoarse and so you took me every year for my birthday. Sadly, due to Covid the Pantomime has been cancelled this year otherwise I would have gone.

You used to spend all year planning my birthday surprise. I miss that. I am greedy and loved to get your gifts. I do not think I will ever get gifts as good as the ones you gave me. This is where I feel unsettled, that feeling of being aware of my own mortality because I am growing one year older and remembering that you will not.

Also because I will have to buy my own gifts from now on, which is not nearly as much fun.

Since we got married in 1992 you have used the same gift bag with a drawing of Mrs Tiggy-Winkle by Beatrix Potter on it for my birthday gift. It took a while to locate it, but I found it and decided that I would buy myself something nice and put it under the tree. My friend Lena from Hitchin has been making the most beautiful watercolour paintings. I saw one on Facebook that really took my fancy. It has a tree with the dregs of autumn—just a few leaves hanging on to its skeletal branches—and a man and his dog further down the path. It seems to capture both loneliness and hope and reminds me of a painting by John Atkinson Grimshaw. And so, in my best Jane Eyre voice, "Reader, I bought it."

And so here I am, warm as toast from the soup, looking at our tree of memories and being thankful for new art for the collection.

All my love,
Heather

Dear Best Beloved,

Despite being devoted Anglophiles who loved British sitcoms (or Britcoms because I do love a portmanteau word!) since arriving in the United Kingdom we have never had a television or a TV Licence. It's not that we haven't watched telly, we just haven't done it at home. When we lived in England you could watch BBC i-player without a licence which made our lives easier. Every Sunday, we would treat ourselves to a packet of crisps and a fizzy drink and go to your school library and watch *Doctor Who*. You said why would we pay for it at home when we could watch it for free at your school? It was easy because Hitchin Boys School was a ten-minute walk from our house.

When we moved to Wales your office was an hour away. We discussed getting a TV Licence, but you came up with a plan. Every six weeks we would pack a picnic lunch and take the bus down all the windy roads to your office in Lampeter where we would snack our way through six episodes of *Doctor Who* and if there was time, any other programme that caught out fancy.

Eventually, the BBC cottoned on to the fact that people were just watching i-player to avoid paying the licence fee and so they made you pay for the privilege. I thought for sure we would get a TV Licence then, but you still held out. You railed about the cost, and you were right. It is frightfully expensive. You said we couldn't afford it and what did I know? I had no idea what our outgoings were until you died. Because money (and the lack thereof) is one of my anxiety triggers, we agreed that you would take charge of that. You would let me know if I wanted to buy something whether it needed to wait until payday. Saying it now makes me feel a bit like, "Don't worry your pretty little head about it" which doesn't sit well with me. But it didn't feel that way at the time and you were never the sort who believed in all that patriarchal nonsense, so I am sure that is not how you meant it. I wish you were here so we could discuss it.

But all this is coming round to telling you that I have bought a TV Licence. Yes, it was expensive. It is £159 a year for the privilege of watching the BBC. Because how else am I going to watch *Doctor Who*? And what if I want to watch other programmes? I can't very well go to your office anymore because you are dead and do not have an office to go to. I know I could do what you did and wait for things to come out on DVD and buy them, but I am tired of being months behind everyone else and having to avoid spoilers. I need some joy in my life and *Doctor Who* keeps me connected to you.

At least they are letting me break it up into manageable monthly payments, which incidentally is something you told me they didn't do. I wonder sometimes if you changed up the facts to suit your own narrative. Perhaps we all do it.

There is a new episode of *Doctor Who* coming out on January 1st, and I will be there watching it at home in my pyjamas while eating snacks. You can join me if you want to.

All my love,
Heather

24/12/2021

Dear Best Beloved,

I think of our Christmas traditions, and I wondered how I would feel as I approach my first Christmas without you. This is one of my favourite times of year. I love the way we celebrated from my birthday on the 11th all the way to the new year.

People told me, "Don't feel like you have to put up a tree this year," and I thought, "Why wouldn't I?" Putting up the tree and looking at all the ornaments brings me such joy. I love the tradition we had of choosing an ornament each December, one for every year we were married. These will remind me how many wonderful years we had together.

The first year we were married, I made us a list of Christmas poems—one for every day in the countdown to Christmas—which I read aloud like a blessing before we ate our evening meal. Every night I would impulsively say, "This is my favourite one!" or "I love this one!" You would laugh and your eyes would crinkle up at the corners and you would say in your mock serious voice, "Really? You've never said." That was your gentle code phrase to tell me that I had indeed said it quite a few times. You had such a good way of gently teasing that was never mean-spirited. But they were all my favourites, and my heart was so full I just had to tell you again.

It's Christmas Eve and I am tucked up in pyjamas all snug as a bug in a rug as you used to say. I've bought the traditional fruits and nuts and candy and some posh vegan cheeses and crackers. I bought that delicious Norfolk punch made with elderberries and herbs and spices that made your tongue numb from the cloves. As I sip it, I think about you singing *All I Want for Christmas Is My Two Front Teeth* with your numbed tongue making you lisp.

Every year we were married we bought a special Christmas card and wrote a message to each other. I have gone through them all tonight and I was struck by your message to me in 1997.

Until the year you died, 1996-1997 was the worst year I had ever experienced. It was my first year of teaching second grade and I was being observed three times a month to qualify for my teaching certificate at the end of the school year. You were diagnosed with stage three Hodgkin's Lymphoma three weeks into the school year, and I had to carry on like it wasn't happening and look after you while trying to teach. All I remember from that year is the sheer panic I felt that you might die. All you remember about that year was feeling sick or being sick and sleeping. You slept like the dead and on more than one occasion I thought you had died because you were so cold and unresponsive. The Christmas of 1996 your Oncologist told me that you were not responding to treatment, and I should treat this Christmas like our last. By the grace of God, you started to show improvement in January of 1997 and made a full recovery. Well, until you died of cancer twenty-four years later.

By Christmas of 1997 you had been in remission for several months. I wrote in the card a message saying how relieved I felt that you had not died and left me alone.

You wrote this back to me:

My Love,
You will never be alone. I am going to fill your life with so much
goodness that if I should leave before you, your heart will be full.

I love you,
Thomas

And you did. You filled my life with so many wonderful shenanigans and adventures that I am indeed filled to the brim from your love. Merry Christmas, Best Beloved.

All my love,
Heather

JANUARY

01/01/2022

Dear Best Beloved,

Happy New Year my darling. Today is one of our many anniversaries. We did love to celebrate, didn't we? It is eighteen years since we arrived in the United Kingdom with six suitcases and a dream. Sometimes I still cannot believe that this is my life.

When we came here as exchange students in 1990, we were filled with a deep longing for a life in this green and pleasant land. Neither of us had ever felt at home in Louisiana—we always felt that something was missing from our lives, but we had no words to describe what it was. We simply knew that we felt empty. This is what was missing. I remember you said that we were like a cactus feeling rain for the first time and blooming when previously we had been barren.

We decided on that trip to get married and emigrate to the United Kingdom. And we did it. We did it together. You always had a way of making me feel brave, making me feel like the impossible was possible. Without you and your love and your belief that we could really do this and live our dream I would not be here. I don't think I would have been brave or clever enough to do it on my own.

People told us it wouldn't work. Your parents tried to talk us out of it. But we knew this is the life we wanted—this is the life we were meant to have. So, here's to you my Best Beloved. I am here and I will continue to live adventurously and keep our dream alive. I am where I have always belonged.

All my love,
Heather

06/01/2022

Dear Best Beloved,

I need some space. I have bought so many books since you died, and they have nowhere to go—every bookshelf in the house is chock-a-block.

You were very clear before you died that I shouldn't be sentimental about your clothes. I should clear them all away as soon as possible and use your clothes rail for my costumes as they had no place to go. In fact, you said I had secretly been sizing up your clothes rail for years which is probably true. You were a minimalist when it came to clothes, and I was always wondering if I could squeeze something like my bulky Anne Boleyn costume made from a set of green curtains at the end of your row of clothes without you noticing. But books are different. I feel like I need to ask your permission to get rid of some of your books.

There are some things that are non-negotiable. I would never get rid of your C.S. Lewis books because I know what he meant to you. But there are others that I have no attachment to and so I hold them in my hand or press them to my heart and see if they "spark joy" as Marie Condo says. Sometimes I open the book to flick through the pages and see if there is any part of you inside and I find that you have stickered it with a bookplate. I remember when you invented a logo for us as a fifteenth wedding anniversary gift. It was beautiful with our names spelled out in a rainbow of colours and included an equally colourful spider illustration. You had the logo printed on bookplates and t-shirts for us that year. When I see a book that you have stickered, even if I want to let it go, I cannot release it if it bears your name. How do I let it go, but still keep it?

The solution came to me in a dream (as so often solutions do) that I should use those books around the house to lift things up. I had been thinking for months that I needed a higher table for our Lumie clock—the clock that wakes you by gradually getting lighter in the morning. The table is so low that I feel the light does not shine bright enough to wake me. But I don't need a higher table, I need to make the table higher. So, now the clock is raised as it sits on three chunky C. S. Lewis biographies. Likewise, the laptop which sits on that low antique desk we bought for my birthday in 2006 needed to be raised. I had been told that it would be more comfortable if the laptop were higher as it would put less strain on my neck when looking at the screen. Now, it sits at just the right height on all those illustrated versions of Kipling's *Just So Stories* that you loved, and I didn't. They are still here and being useful, but now there is space on the shelves for my books.

I think that is a good compromise, don't you think?

All my love,
Heather

22/01/2022

Dear Best Beloved,

I dreamt of you last night. I know it was you, but I couldn't see your sweet face. It was as if you were always standing in the shadows. In the dream I readjusted my position several times to try to see you more clearly and each time you pulled yourself further away. I was afraid I might lose you again and so I let you stay cloaked in darkness to be able to hold onto you.

You said to me, "Well, it looks like you have it all figured out. Work at the bookshop, write stories, make art, travel, and then retire. Sounds like you have it all planned. I guess you don't need me anymore."

"Of course I need you!" I cried. "There are still heavy things to be carried!" How we laughed at that. But I sensed you were serious. That somehow, I had planned out my whole future and none of it included you. I guess I have.

I tried to think of ways that I still needed you, but everything I listed I had learned to do myself over these last ten months. Maybe I didn't need you anymore. I realised you might be able to read my mind and I quickly flooded my brain with thoughts about you and me and all the ways I still need you—still ache for you—still desperately want you by my side. You reached out your hand from the darkness and touched my heart. Then you were gone.

I thought that my heart was illuminated after your touch. I could see a bright white light emanating from my chest. It lit the room. But then suddenly the alarm went off and I realised that what I thought was my light was simply the Lumie clock. Since I have raised it with your books, I can see it better.

I used to feel that I was the lamp, and you were my light. That it was your love that illuminated me from within. I had been afraid since you died that I had lost my light, that my light had dimmed so much that it might go out and you would not be here to fill my lamp. Perhaps I still have my spark. Perhaps I can still shine. Perhaps it never left me. Perhaps, perhaps, perhaps.

All my love,
Heather

26/01/2022

Dear Best Beloved,

Today I did that thing I sometimes do where I exaggerate to prove a point. I take a truth and I make it a lie by the fact that it is inflated. You used to hate it when I did this. You would whip your head round, fix me with a steely gaze and declare, "Heather Elizabeth Tisdale, BE BETTER."

I don't even know why I did it. The moment the words spilled out of my mouth like sewage I was horrified, and I could feel you judging me from beyond the grave. I am so sorry to have let you down. I am sorry to have let myself down. It was easier when you were alive because we held each other to a high standard and if the other person needed to be better, we let them know.

So, I just wanted to say that I heard you and that right now you are a better person dead than I am alive, but I will try. You have my word.

All my love,
Heather

27/01/2022

Dear Best Beloved,

Last year on this day was the last normal day before our world came crashing down. I had an appointment for a mammogram in the mobile unit in the Morrisons Supermarket car park. I was nervous. Nervous about the actual procedure—so many women in my family have had breast cancer. I was nervous about getting there because it involved a bus. With a bus, you must know where to get off. What if I missed my stop? And then, the even more difficult bit, where do you wait to get the return bus because it is never in the same place where the bus dropped you off. I needed you to go with me.

You had finally admitted to me that you felt something wasn't right. That the stitch in your right side was more than a stitch. You were famously a terrible communicator over the phone and so I made you tell me in detail everything that hurt, and I wrote all your symptoms down with bullet points so that you could refer to it when you phoned St Peter's Surgery to speak to our GP.

Then you procrastinated for three days while my anxiety spiralled. What if by the time you got around to phoning, they wanted to see you on the same day and time that I had my mammogram appointment?

On the morning of the 27th, you woke up and had a bath. You hadn't bathed in nearly two weeks because you said there was no point as you were working from home, but later admitted to me it was because you were afraid you were too weak to climb out of the bath. You were bright and cheerful. You made me laugh with your description of a mammogram as a "boob sandwich between two panes of glass." You seemed completely normal, better than you had in weeks. We took the bus, and you pottered around the supermarket while I had the procedure done. You came out of Morrisons with a bottle of elderflower cordial. A treat you said for being a good patient. We bussed home and as we climbed the stairs, I saw you visibly deflate. You looked like a balloon with a slow leak. I could see with my own eyes that you were seriously unwell. I realised that for my sake you had pulled yourself together because I needed you. You had mustered every ounce of strength you had because I was feeling weak.

You protested that it was too late in the day to phone the doctor, but I insisted. You got a phone call-back and then downplayed all the symptoms I had helpfully bullet-pointed, and you tried to "shush" me as I shouted things like, "Tell her about the terrible pain in your side!" loudly in the background. She must have heard me because she ordered you to come to the surgery the next day and have a blood test. And that was it.

I think about this day, the last good thing you did for me before you sickened and died. I can't remember if I thanked you at the time so I shall do it now. Thank you for looking after me, even though you should have been looking after you.

All my love,
Heather

FEBRUARY

01/02/2022

Dear Best Beloved,

It's the beginning of the end today. Last year on the first day of February we got the phone call that would change our lives forever. At 5 p.m. our GP rang up and said your bloodwork results had come back and were very alarming. You needed to go straight to hospital. They were expecting you. Go. Go now. Pack a bag. She thought you would be home in a few days. It turned out to be nineteen days.

We asked if I could go with you, just to get you settled in or speak with a doctor, but because of Covid I wasn't allowed. You packed a bag while I ran out to the cashpoint to get money for a taxi. We hugged on the pavement outside the house while the taxi driver waited patiently and then you were gone.

And forty-five days later, you were really gone.

I am feeling it today, as keenly as I did last year. The fear. The anxiety. The sadness. But not the hope because this time I know how it ends.

All my love,
Heather

13/02/2022

Dear Best Beloved,

It's your birthday today. You were never one for celebrating, not when it was your birthday. For me you would spend all year planning some elaborate surprise, but when it was your special day, you didn't want any fuss. I finally convinced you to let me celebrate because every birthday you had was another year that we had been in love. Another year of growing older together. Now I am the only one who will grow old.

We used to laugh that we were only the same age for two months of the year. We were both born in 1969, but you came into this world at the beginning and I arrived at the very end of the year. From December to February, we would be the same age and then you would become older than me once again and I would spend the whole rest of the year catching up.

But today, we are still the same age because you won't get any older. You should be fifty-three today, but you remain forever fifty-two. Next year I will be the oldest one. You will be the one trailing behind me.

It feels wrong, like the world has gone askew on its axis when I grow old, and you do not. This is not how it was supposed to be. We were meant to grow old together. So, my love, I must take the slow path. I am still right behind you and someday will catch you up again. But not for a long time.

I will keep your light alive until we meet again.

All my love,
Heather

Dear Best Beloved,

It is Valentine's Day today. We both used to humph about the commercialism of this holiday as if showing someone you loved them and buying them treats was something a person was only obligated to do once a year. Though we both used to love to scoop up bargain chocolates the day after.

I wasn't planning on doing anything special today. However, I was doom-scrolling on YouTube when I saw a trailer for a most interesting film. There was a new version of *Cyrano De Bergerac* starring Peter Dinklage as the title character. Instead of Cyrano being self-conscious about his nose in this version it is his height. I quickly checked the cinema listings and lo and behold it was showing locally tonight at 7 p.m.

I go to the cinema quite a lot. I think I have been more times since you died than in all the years that we have lived in the United Kingdom. I don't know what put us off going in the past. Probably money. I am sure the tickets cost more when we lived in England. Plus, we had to take the train to Letchworth as Hitchin didn't have a cinema and so we had to factor in transportation costs as well. I now have mastered the skill of buying cinema tickets by myself and if I buy my ticket online it only costs £4.99 for a regular show. That's a bargain and only a ten-minute walk from our house.

I think the real reason I go to the cinema so much is because it is the place that I seem to catch a glimpse of you the most. I can often see you like a shadow in my peripheral vision, and it comforts me to know that you are there watching it with me.

Tonight, I was surprised by the appearance of the actor Richard McCabe who was playing the role of the Priest. We have avidly followed his career since we saw him as Puck in *A Midsummer Night's Dream* in 1990. I was so surprised, I quickly turned to the seat next to me with my mouth agape and I saw you. I saw you as clear as day. Not a shadow. Not a glimmer. But you were as real as if you were alive and sitting by my side. We both looked surprised—partly because we saw Richard McCabe, but mostly because we saw each other. I turned back to the screen and tried to keep you in my side eye, but you had gone back to being a ghost. But I am so thankful that you made an appearance, however briefly.

All my love,
Heather

Dear Best Beloved,

It is February 20th. The day we met. The day that changed my life.

It was 1989. John David was having a birthday. I knew him from high school. You knew him from RA camp where you two had been counsellors together and Lottie knew him because their dads were friends.

Lottie invited me to the party that was being held at Louisiana College, in the common room of English Village. This was a Baptist party so there was no loud music, dancing, and drinking. It was more of a Scrabble and cake sort of party.

I was feeling a bit bored by the whole party business because I love to dance and there wasn't going be any dancing here. When the Scrabble board arrived and was met with an enthusiastic cheer, I knew it was time to go home.

I do not play Scrabble.

But then, I heard it. A voice. A voice singing. A voice singing FRANK ZAPPA. I thought, "Who in this Baptist college knows Frank Zappa besides me?" I heard it again. *Ship arriving too late to save a drowning witch.* It was not a mistake. I looked frantically around to see who it was, and it was you.

Now, I had known you for a whole semester and we had gone on many group outings together, but not once had I ever heard you speak. You were always polite and did things like held the door open for me or brought me another glass of grape juice at lunch, but had I ever heard you speak aloud? No, I had not. You were shy.

I asked you later why Frank Zappa and all you could say was, "I could tell you were about to go, and I had to do something to make you stay."

So, we walked away (far away) from the Scrabble game and sat by ourselves.

This is where the magic happened.

We talked. We talked and talked and laughed and laughed. We discussed the Romantic poets. You liked Keats and Shelley, I fancied Wordsworth (whom you called Turdsworth which made me snort), but we both could agree on Coleridge. We quoted our favourite parts of *The Rime of the Ancient Mariner* to each other. We recited the entire "dead parrot sketch" from *Monty Python* and I laughed until I fell off the sofa.

The air crackled. I could feel myself falling in love. Honestly, like all those clichéd films where Cupid comes out and shoots someone in the heart and little cartoon hearts blip and twinkle above their heads. It was like that.

I suddenly had this idea that I really needed to make a good impression. The more excitable I get, the less dignified I am. I start to flap my hands like an insane goose trying to fly south for the winter. So,

I thought of a solution.

Cake. I could have a slice of cake. If I was holding a plate and a fork, I could not flap like I was trying to fly to the moon. So, I had a slice of cake.

It was all going so well. We talked about music and were going through the entire catalogue of Peter, Paul, and Mary songs. I was telling you about when I was a child, how I dressed up with my apron wrapped about me and pretended to be accidentally mistaken for a swan and shot with an arrow by my sweetheart like the song *Polly Von* when someone said:

"Where's the cake?"

I realised, to my horror, that I had eaten the ENTIRE birthday cake. I had eaten it all myself. Eight slices. In front of you.

I had tried to be dignified and instead had made an utter tit of myself. I burned with shame.

In my defence, it was a German Chocolate Cake.

I asked you later what you thought as you saw me go back for slice after slice of cake. You replied that you couldn't believe such a tiny person could pack away that much food. It was apparently pretty impressive.

I recovered my composure and hid my plate under the sofa. We continued to talk, and I wondered if I had blown it. You could never love someone like me. It was many years later that I found out that you already liked me. Ever since you saw me in the play *Tartuffe* in

1988. You had liked me for a whole year and been too shy to talk to me. That's why you didn't want me to leave. Hence the Frank Zappa.

At about 3 a.m., it was time to go back to our respective dormitories.

You hugged Lottie goodbye.

You hugged her roommate Lisa goodbye, in what I judged to be longer than the hug you gave Lottie. You always said this wasn't so. You said you hardly knew Lisa. I was mortified. What if all night you had been forced to talk to the mad cake eating woman who flapped her arms and threatened you with a fork if you dared leave the sofa?

I nearly started to cry. Because, you see, I loved you. I loved you already.

Then you hugged me. I was so ashamed that I tried to pull away and you wouldn't let me. You held me in those strong arms, and I melted. The whole rest of the world faded away and we were actually in the night sky surrounded by stars. I know that sounds like a crap metaphor for love in a badly written romance novel, but it is true. Every word. We hugged for ages until someone went, "Oooooo," and everyone laughed. We broke apart and began to walk back to our dorms.

As we walked along the boardwalk, my feet didn't touch the ground. I know that is also a well-worn cliché, but it is 100% true. I looked down and I was levitating slightly. Hand on heart, that really happened.

We got back to Cottingham, and we were all going to have a slumber party in one dorm room. Everyone else was tired, but I was wide awake. It looked something like this:

Me: "Wasn't he wonderful? He's so funny and clever. Do you think he likes me??"

Everyone else: "Shut up and go to sleep, it's almost four in the morning!!!"

The next day, self-doubt kept creeping in. I felt like you were my soulmate, but did you feel the same way? I was suddenly tongue-tied. Thankfully Lottie knew what to do.

Basically, she did the grown-up equivalent of that eighth-grade game:

Do you like Heather?
Circle one
Yes   No

She phoned you up and asked you. I was in the TV room watching *The Comic Strip Presents*. It was the episode *Consuela, or the new Mrs Saunders*. Lisa came flying through the double doors and screamed, "He likes you! He says he likes you!"

And that was it really.

From that day in 1989 until your untimely death last March we were inseparable. So, I give thanks and I would not trade you for the world.

To quote Shakespeare's Sonnet 29:

> *For thy sweet love remembered such wealth brings*
> *that then I scorn to change my state with kings.*

All my love,
Heather

Dear Best Beloved,

In February of 2020 we had the best holiday of our lives. It was a real bucket list of a trip. We had been saying for years we wanted to do it, but always got sucked back into the lure of London and never did. I am so glad that we did because a month later the world was in the grip of the pandemic, and everything was shut down. We had no idea that it would be the last vacation we would ever take, so I am thankful we made it a good one.

It had been thirty years since we had been exchange students in 1990 and we wanted to celebrate with all the things we loved from that trip. It was perfectly us.

We had to get to Somerset by public transportation which made it a bit like *Around the World in Eighty Days* with all the modes of transportation used. You joked that the only thing we were missing was a hot air balloon. Eventually we arrived at Cricket St Thomas which was the very posh manor house that was used as the location for *Grantleigh Manor* in the Britcom *To the Manor Born*. We spent the week with you regaling me with your hilarious impression of Penelope Keith as the snooty character of Audrey fforbes-Hamilton. I think I laughed more on that trip than I had all year.

We arranged for a lovely local taxi driver to take us around places we wanted to go, and I am so glad we did because by the end of the week "Paul the Taxi" (as he was known in his village) became a trusted friend.

We wanted this trip to be all about science and literature. We thought it would be appropriate since our LC/MC exchange experience included both English literature with Dr Connie Douglas and the history of science with Dr Ted Snazelle.

We spent a glorious sunny day in the town of Lyme Regis on the Jurassic Coast. The first thing we did was go to the local museum to learn about Mary Anning the English fossil collector, dealer, and palaeontologist. Her findings contributed to important changes in scientific thinking about prehistoric life and the history of the Earth. Sadly, she was never admitted to the Geological Society in London due to being a woman. We sat on the rocky beach eating chips and warding off seagulls while we railed against the patriarchy. This is just one of the many things I loved about you, the way you were so passionate about standing up against injustice, even one that happened over a hundred years ago, I bought a small ammonite fossil as a souvenir and every time I look at it, I remember this trip and what it was like to be happy with you.

Then we walked to The Cobb which was featured in Jane Austen's final book *Persuasion*. It is here that Louisa Musgrove made her impetuous leap and brained herself after insisting that Captain Wentworth catch her as she jumped down. I lay down on the ground, body splayed as if I had fallen, and recreated her ridiculous act while you took photos of me. You kept saying, "Oh dear! Miss Musgrove! Whatever have you done!" as other tourists wandered by wondering what in the world was happening. As I was lying there, I overheard this conversation:

Confused man: "Why is she lying on the ground?"

Exasperated woman: "Because it's Jane Austen, dear." (heavy sigh)

In 2013 our friend Chris casually said, "Have you ever been to Watchet? It's where Coleridge wrote the *Ancient Mariner*. There is a statue of the Mariner with the albatross around his neck by the harbour. Oh, and you can stand in the forest and hear the sea." This offhand comment lodged in my heart, and I have thought of it often. The next day we got to make that dream come true.

We took a very long taxi ride with our delightful taxi man to the town of Watchet (which is just fun to say as it sounds like "Watch it!") and the first thing we saw in the harbour was the beautiful statue, I had no idea that an albatross was so enormous. We sat on the green grass in the bright glare of the sunshine and talked about Coleridge, just like we did on the night we met because we were geeks even then. I would start our favourite quotes and you would finish them, and it felt like we were perfectly in tune with each other.

We started to talk about how Coleridge's most famous portrait makes him look a bit toady.

So, you said, "And now *The Wind in the Willows* starring the Romantic Poets!" which made me laugh so hard I snorted. Then we spent a good half hour deciding who was who. The results were:

Badger—Wordsworth
Mole—Keats
Ratty—Shelley
Mr Toad—Coleridge

And Byron probably thought he was Pan, but he was more like The Wayfarer, the vagabond sea faring rat.

Then we walked the clifftops and into the woods and stood in silence as we held hands and listened to the soporific sounds of the sea.

I am so glad that I have this one last good memory of you when we were so happy before 2020 happened and the whole world fell apart and then 2021 when my personal world came crashing down.

I always think of you when I read these lines from Coleridge's poem:

> *He prayeth best, who loveth best*
> *All things both great and small;*
> *For the dear God who loveth us,*
> *He made and loveth all.*

All my love,
Heather

MARCH

01/03/2022

Dear Best Beloved,

One year ago today we saw the Oncologist. One year ago today we had hope, didn't we? I remember how frightened you were about the prospect of chemotherapy again. You cried on the morning of the appointment because you didn't think you could bear to go through it a second time. I had never seen you so upset. You just kept saying that you were going to beg the doctor to give you weaker chemotherapy for longer than be blasted with it for a short time and be so sick and exhausted. That was the plan.

I remember showing up to the appointment prepared. I had a notebook and a pen because I was going to write down all the important information. I remember that you went into the consultation room first and I wanted to ask you to swap places so I could write with my left hand and hold your hand on the right. But I didn't.

I remember the way the doctor looked at us when you asked about chemotherapy. I will never forget her face when she realised that we didn't know. That we had no idea that you were dying and there was no hope. She just kept saying, "The hospital should have explained it to you. When they said you were to have chemotherapy it was only for palliative care to give you a few more months before you die." Months. She said you had months to live. She was wrong. You had weeks. Seventeen days. That made you furious. You did not go gentle into that good night. I remember in your last days of life before you lost the ability to communicate that you were white hot with rage against the dying of the light as you shouted, "She promised us months!"

It was so awful, but I was relieved for you that you did not have to endure chemotherapy again since you were terrified of it. That was the only blessing out of this sorry mess of a situation.

So here I am again at the start of your end. It hurts today as keenly as it did then. Your last days were difficult and painful, but I did the best I could to ease your passing. I miss you and my life will never be quite the same without you, but I am slowly moving forward. Counting my steps on the path that leads me back to you.

All my love,
Heather

10/03/2022

Dear Best Beloved,

Now that it has been almost a year since you died people have been asking me when I plan to date again. "You're young!" they say. Yes, I am. I am far too young to be widowed. But that doesn't mean I want to get married again. When I tell them the truth that no one could measure up to you they dismiss my claim with a wave of their hand and exclaim, "Well, it's early days yet. You may change your mind. You never know what life has in store for you!" I find it offensive that they would even suggest it and even more infuriating that they think I don't know what is best for myself.

You suggested it. When you were dying you told me that you wanted me to be happy and if I found someone else you would be glad because you didn't want me to be lonely.

But here's the thing—I am not lonely. Over this last year I have embraced solitude and have found joy in having the house to myself. In fact, I love it. At first the house seemed to echo with the emptiness and lack of you, but over time I realised that it resonates with your frequency. You are everywhere. All the things I love from the art on the walls to the books on the shelves to our beautiful unconventional pets remind me of you. If I met someone else, I would have to compromise. Perhaps they would want to hang some of their own art on my walls or put their own books on my shelf or maybe they have arachnophobia. In this last year I have lost the ability to share. It doesn't mean I am selfish it just means I discovered that I need my own space.

Don't feel like cooking? Cereal for supper is acceptable if you live alone and I can even leave the bowl in the sink overnight to be washed up in the morning. Leaving my shoes in the middle of the floor is fine because there is nobody else here to complain about tripping over them. I currently have an art project going on in every room of this house and I don't need to tidy them away because I am sharing the space with someone else.

I have friends who meet all my emotional and social needs. I don't need a romantic partner to do that.

You were the best person for me, and we were a great team but now I like being my own person. I do not need a partner to complete me. It has taken all this time to truly understand that I am enough.

All my love,
Heather

16/03/2022

Dear Best Beloved,

I cannot believe that last year at this time it was your last night on this Earth. For days you had been so agitated and restless, always trying to get up in the middle of the night and then falling because your body was giving up even though your mind was still trying to fight. Several nights in a row I had to call the emergency helpline and have nurses come and help me lift you back into bed. I was too afraid to sleep because you needed to be cared for and I was alone.

On this night last year, a Marie Curie nurse was sent to sit with you all night so that I could rest. She arrived around 10 p.m. I remember that she got lost and I had to go out on the street in front of the house and wave to her. They must have known that you were very close to death. I didn't realise it at the time just how close you were. I had no idea when she arrived that in five hours and thirty-seven minutes you would take your last breath.

I set her up with a chair in our bedroom and then she told me to go sleep on the sofa and she would come get me if your circumstances changed. I remember how blissful it was to finally be able to relax knowing someone else was looking out for you. I remember when she came to wake me.

"It's time," she said.

"So soon?" I asked.

"Come now." She replied.

So, I did. I wasn't sure how long we would have. In the end it was about forty-five minutes. I wondered if your life was flashing before your eyes or if that was only something that only happened in films. I told you our story about the wonderful life we shared and hoped you could hear me. I did a lot of singing, mostly songs that included the word "heather" in them like *Wild Mountain Thyme* and *Scarborough Fair*. Your breathing became more rapid, you were gasping and straining for each breath. I hoped you weren't in pain, but there was no way for you to tell me if you were. All I could think of was, "Your suffering will soon be over." I sang our wedding song and you let out one last violent gasp and then you were gone for good.

Oh, Best Beloved I am so glad you are at peace but tonight it is me who is restless and agitated as I remember our last moments together and feel the heartache of letting you go all over again.

All my love,
Heather

17/03/2021

Dear Best Beloved,

It's "Saint Thomas Day" today. The day you got your wings.

I always thought I would die of a broken heart if you were to leave me. Do you remember the way I used to follow you around when we were first married begging you to promise that you would not die before me? You were wise oh Best Beloved to tell me that you could not make that promise. When you got cancer four years later, I thought I was being punished by God for asking you not to die before me. When you were dying you said to me, "We always knew it would probably be me first," and you were right. I did. I just tried very hard to pretend that it would never happen.

I truly believed that I loved you so much that I would not be able to go on without you. I thought that my heart would stop beating, that the grief would be so painful that my heart would just give up. It didn't.

For days and weeks after you died, the pain in my solar plexus was agony, but still I lived. Grief tore me apart and I cried like Alice in Wonderland creating a pool of tears, but I didn't drown.

Every time I cursed you for leaving me alone, I could hear your voice saying:

You're braver than you think and stronger than you know.

And so, I have concluded that I am here to stay. That God still has work for me to do on this Earth and I can spend all my time in the past thinking about what I lost, or I can go forward in your memory and try to do some good in the world. I would rather do it with you, but that is not the choice I have been given. So, I will carry on your compassionate legacy, and I will create a life of joy, even if it is not the life I had envisioned. I hope that by telling our story it will become a survival guide for someone else who is lost in grief. Maybe something good can come out of this tragedy.

All my love,
Heather

ALSO BY THIS AUTHOR

Wounds: New Openings Into Old Stories

ACKNOWLEDGEMENTS

First a huge thank you and my undying gratitude to Ingram Publishing because you have created a template programme that does all the setting of margins and other complicated mathematical things thus making ADOBE redundant. I literally could not have made this book without you.

Thank you to Sasin Tipchai (Sasint from Pixabay) for the gorgeous cover art that expresses the longing in my soul so well.

Thank you to my dearest friends who have held me up as I struggled to make sense of this tragedy—Cheryl and Nigel, Jo, Karen, Priya, Emma, Kirsty, Carole and RM, Soong, Helen and the Shenanigans Gang, Paul and the staff at Tea Traders and so many more. Thank you. Special thanks to Gloria: you have been a role model for me for much of my life, but especially since Thomas died. You lost your husband about the age that I am now and even though your heart was broken, you learned to fly again and travel and have many adventures. This is the future I want for myself.

To my dear old mum, who was tragically killed in a car accident on the 31st of July 2022. Now you are both late in the time sense and the dead sense. I am sorry you didn't live to see this book published. You were a great example of resilience after losing two husbands to cancer. You showed me is was possible to go on.

Thanks to the band The Decemberists for the title of the book from their most excellent song. If you don't know this band, I would urge you to check them out. They are the best storytellers I know. I highly recommend starting with "The Mariner's Revenge Song."

The poem "Longing" by Matthew Arnold was first published in 1852 in the book *Empedocles on Etna, and Other Poems*. "The Rime of the Ancient Mariner" by Samuel Taylor Coleridge was first published in the book *Lyrical Ballads* in 1798, and Sonnet 29 by William Shakespeare was first published in 1609. All three poems are in the public domain.

In case you were wondering:

Mina Murray is from the book *Dracula* by Bram Stoker. The trolley is black and white like a chess board that reminded me of Murray Head singing "One Night in Bangkok" from the musical *Chess*. Somehow, Murray Head morphed into Mina Murray. Zeppelin is named for the band Led Zeppelin and their song "Stairway to Heaven." Stephen Fryer named after national treasure Stephen Fry whom we met once when Thomas blagged us backstage passes after a recording of the television programme *Q.I.* because it was our anniversary. Hester Prynne is from Nathaniel Hawthorne's book *The Scarlet Letter*. Ionesco is named for the absurdist play *The Chairs* by playwright Eugene Ionesco. Lastly, Little Tom Dacre is named for the sorrowful young chimney sweep in William Blake's *Songs of Innocence, Songs of Experience*.

If you want to read more about the time Thomas was interviewed by the BBC about William Blake, check out this link: *www.bbc.co.uk/news/education-22971225*

If you are intrigued by all the storytellings I mentioned, please visit the YouTube Channel for Goldstone Books at *www.youtube.com/@goldstonebooks4233* or go to YouTube and search *Goldstone Books*.

For many years Thomas volunteered at RAMA—Refuge for Aged and Mistreated Animals. He is buried at the back of their field. They are a wonderful sanctuary who rescues and cares for animals. If you want to know more about the work that they do and how you can support them, please visit their website at *https://ramasfamily.wixsite.com/ramasfamily*

And at the very end, I will thank you my Best Beloved. I am sorry that I have to thank you for this, but without your untimely end there would be no book. I wish with all my heart I did not have to write it, but I do and so I hope that my journey will somehow help others who are caught in the darkness of grief. I hope that this shows them there is a way back to the Light.

ABOUT THE AUTHOR

Heather Tisdale was born and raised in Louisiana. She has always had a flair for the dramatic and has been spinning tales from the moment she could speak. She graduated twice from Louisiana College, once with a degree that made her an interesting and well-rounded person and then went back to get her teaching qualification because being an interesting and well-rounded person does not get you a job. While in college she and her sidekick (who later became her husband) were exchange students for three months in London and became devoted Anglophiles. In 2004 they decided to live adventurously by leaving the American South and moving to the United Kingdom. She lived for a decade in England and now resides in a crooked pink house in rainy Wales after the untimely death of her beloved husband. She is an author, an artist and an activist.

Ingram Content Group UK Ltd.
Milton Keynes UK
UKHW040706200323
418846UK00001B/138

9 781916 198913